HEAVEN:

THE 3 PHASES OF
GOD'S ETERNAL PLAN

JASON B. DENNETT

www.xulonpress.com

Acknowledgements:

To Jon and Carmen, for their "push"
and friendly encouragement.

To Pastor Dan, for all the years of patient training,
excellent mentoring, and Christ-centered
discipleship. All I am today in ministry,
I owe to you.

To my beautiful bride Gina, without whose
unwavering support, constant encouragement,
and unfailing love, this never would have
happened. You fill my life with color,
agape love, and the beauty of Jesus.

To Jesus Christ, the Lord of Heaven, Savior of my
soul, and the Great Hero of my heart.

Table of Contents:

Chapter 1

Hungering for Heaven

I n 1952, Florence Chadwick was in the process of setting a new world record: swimming 26 miles in the open ocean. You see, Florence Chadwick was one of the world's most famous "open ocean" swimmers. By this time in 1952, she had already set world records by crossing the English Channel in record time...twice. Her first time, she navigated the English Channel from the shores of England to France in just 13 hours. The second time Florence accomplished this amazing feat, swimming against the current, she crossed from France back over to England in just over 16 hours. This double achievement made her the first female swimmer in history, to cross the English Channel both ways.

But now, Florence Chadwick was about to embark on another jaw-dropping feat: performing a 26 mile open ocean swim, from the west coast of California to the island of Catalina! To make matters worse, the waters off the coast of California can be bone-numbingly cold and shark infested! But none of this deterred the iron-willed athlete, Florence Chadwick. For months on end she had been training to prepare her body for the frigid waters and the dangerously grueling swim to Catalina Island. She was determined to conquer the water, and to set a new world record yet again.

When the fateful day of her record-breaking swim arrived, she embarked into the water surrounded by a team of paramedics, medical professionals, and was even followed by her very own mother in the floating entourage. The purpose of this medical and support team was to protect Florence from any possible shark attack, but also to give any medical assistance necessary over the course of her grueling swim.

After Florence had been swimming for over 15 hours, things took a turn for the worse. A huge bank of fog rolled over the water and was so intense that the entire team was disoriented, and Florence was no longer sure of her position relative to the shore. As if this wasn't bad enough, she began to be overcome by muscular exhaustion, fatigue, and possible hypothermia. She was utterly confused in the water, not sure of her position or direction, and her emotions began to crack under the strain of the mounting circumstances. Eventually, Florence began to cry uncontrollably, fearing that she no longer had the stamina to complete her swim, and terrified that she wouldn't be able to make it to the finish.

Her mother and her personal doctor tried desperately to encourage Florence and buoy her hopes, but to no avail. Florence, after being disoriented by the fog, and overcome by physical exhaustion, made the difficult decision to quit her swim. She was pulled out of the water, placed in the medical boat, and lovingly wrapped in a blanket. The team, still lost and confused in the fog bank, now attempted to determine their position and distance from the shoreline.

As her team navigated their way through the dense embankment of fog and mist, they finally managed to emerge from it. They discovered to their horror, that Florence had quit her swim within only 1 mile of the shoreline! Surrounded by the fog, and unable to keep the shore in view, she had given up within the reach of her ultimate goal.

Later, when Florence attended a press conference covering her attempt at a new world record, she made this comment regarding her decision:

"I think I could've made it, if only I could have seen the shore."

This story of Florence Chadwick, adapted from Randy Alcorn's book "Heaven", aptly illustrates the struggle that many Christians are facing today: they also feel like quitting and giving up, since they can't truly see the "shoreline" of Heaven.

Surrounded by the fog of life, and engulfed in the mists of problems and tribulations, many Christians simply feel like they should give up on their walk with Christ, and throw in the spiritual towel. Discouragement, depression, and spiritual warfare, seem to afflict a large number of Christians to such a degree that they feel despondent, detached, and apathetic towards the things of God. I believe that the solution to this dilemma is partially found by rediscovering, or perhaps discovering for the very first time, the biblical truth and amazing reality of Heaven!

Unbeknownst to the majority of Christians today, and even many Christian pastors, is that the topic of Heaven used to be a main focus in pulpits throughout America's churches centuries ago. A casual reading of older sermons from Reformation preachers like Martin Luther, to the times of Charles Spurgeon in the 1800's, reveals that the topic of Heaven was a regular theme in many Christian churches.

As seagoing captains turned to the North Star to help them navigate their ships at night time through treacherous and dangerous waters, so the Christian church of the past centuries regularly turned to the biblical doctrine of Heaven, to help them navigate the trials and tribulations of this earthly life. The teaching of Heaven was a precious truth that regularly guided, inspired, and motivated believers of the past centuries to live rightly, serve diligently, and prepare eternally for the imminent arrival of the Kingdom of God – Heaven!

Listen to a short sampling from the "Prince of Preachers", Charles Spurgeon, perhaps the greatest preacher of the 1800's, and what he had to say about Heaven:

"If there were no hell, the loss of Heaven would itself be hell!"

"You remember the story of the three wonders in heaven. The first wonder was that we should

see so many there we did not expect to see. The second was that we should miss so many we did expect to see there. But the third wonder would be the greatest wonder of all...to see ourselves there."

"There is a crown there which nobody's head but yours can ever wear. There is a seat in which none but yourself can sit. There is a harp that will be silenced till your fingers strike its strings. There is a robe, made for you, which no one else can wear, waiting for you...So they are waiting and watching for you."

"I suspect that every saved soul of Heaven is a great wonder, and that Heaven is a vast Museum of wonders, grace, and mercy, a palace of miracles, in which everything will surprise everyone who gets there."

"I believe that Heaven is a fellowship of the saints, and that we shall know one another there... I reckon on meeting David, whose songs have so often cheered my soul. I want to meet with Martin Luther and Calvin, and to have the power of seeing such men as Whitfield and Wesley, and walking and talking with them in the golden streets."

If that short sampling does not impress you, then listen to the words of other great Christian minds down through the centuries, speaking on this fascinating topic of Heaven in their own words:

"Our way to Heaven lies through the wilderness of this world...Earth is embittered to us, in order that Heaven may be endeared"
- Matthew Henry
"Commentary on the whole Bible" (1706)

"I do not know how near it may be to us; it may be that some of us will be ushered very soon into the presence of the King. One gaze at Him will be enough to reward us for all we have had to bear. Yes, there is peace with the past, grace with the present, and glory for the future."
- D. L. Moody
"12 Select Sermons" (1884)

"Heaven is as near to our souls, as this world is to our bodies; and we are created, we are redeemed, to have our living in it."
- William Law
"The Spirit of Prayer" (1750)

"Heaven is not a state of mind. Heaven is reality itself."
- C. S. Lewis
"The Great Divorce" (1946)

"I want to know one thing–the way to Heaven; how to land safe on that happy shore."
- John Wesley
"Sermons on Several Occasions" (18th century)

Though these earlier and powerful preachers seem to have regularly thought upon and wrote about the biblical doctrine of Heaven, this seems to be the exception today in many of our modern churches. Heaven just isn't something that most pastors tend to speak about during a typical Sunday service.

Nonetheless, we still have many of the same questions today that our brothers and sisters did centuries ago, concerning the doctrine of Heaven. Chances are, that you yourself have asked these very same questions from time to time. Heavenly "brain teasers" such as:

"What will life truly be like in Heaven?"

*"Will we be able to eat food in
Heaven? What kinds?"*

"Will there be animals in Heaven?"

*"What will we look like in Heaven? Will we have
physical bodies?"*

*"Will Heaven be boring? What will there be
to do for all eternity?"*

*"Will we recognize and know each
other in Heaven?"*

"Will we still be married in Heaven?"

"Will we have special jobs to do in Heaven?"

"Will our bodies have special abilities or supernatural powers?"

"Will we truly live forever in Heaven?"

"Will we see God face to face in Heaven?"

Hopefully these questions, and many more, will be answered throughout the course of this book. However, in order to answer these questions, we need to turn to special portions of Scripture that deal specifically with this wonderful and surprising topic of Heaven. To begin our study, we'll start by examining the third chapter of the book of Colossians, and what Paul tells them about God's eternal plan.

By way of introduction, if you aren't very familiar with this small book of Colossians, it packs a big theological punch! The theme of Colossians is short and sweet: *Jesus is all you really need!* The Colossians, like many Christians today, were being tempted to be made "more complete" in their standing with God by adding works, mysticism, or academic knowledge to their spirituality. Paul tells them boldly and clearly, that if they have Christ, they are complete and need nothing else. *"Jesus plus nothing!"* is the great battle-cry of this wonderful New Testament letter.

To briefly give you an understanding of the flow of Colossians, in chapter 1, Paul teaches us the *"Truth about the CHRIST."* Here, he describes in breathtaking detail 10 amazing descriptions of the Divinity and Deity of Jesus Christ. He declares unflinchingly that Jesus is the God-Man that came to save us!

In chapter 2, Paul moves on and teaches us the ***"Truth about the CULTS."*** Here he denounces the spiritual pitfalls that were seeking to overthrow the early Christians in Colossae, such as legalism, mysticism, and pseudo-intellectualism. He instructs them to leave these things behind since they are already fully complete by Christ indwelling them!

Lastly, in chapters 3 and 4, he explains to us the ***"Truth about the CHRISTIAN."*** This is where Paul shows how their *doctrine* should be lived out in their *deeds*; how their *beliefs* should be evidenced in their *behavior*. He takes the truths of the first two chapters, and shows the believers how that should look in their personal purity, in family relationships, in the workplace, and relating to the world around them.

However, when Paul begins his instruction about what the Christian life should look like practically, he surprisingly anchors it in the marvelous truth of Heaven. In other words, the very first practical consideration that Paul mentions for the Christian, is to be living for Heaven! He says that *this* is the first order of business of living out the truth of who Christ is, and what He's done in our lives.

Let's take a moment and read the first four verses of Colossians chapter 3, in multiple Bible translations, to get the full color and meaning of the text:

Colossians 3:1-4 NKJV

"If then you were raised with Christ, seek those things which are above, where Christ is, sitting at the right hand of God. Set your mind on things above, not on things on the earth. For you

died, and your life is hidden with Christ in God. When Christ [who is] our life appears, then you also will appear with Him in glory."

Colossians 3:1-4 NLT

"Since you have been raised to new life with Christ, set your sights on the realities of heaven, where Christ sits in the place of honor at God's right hand. Think about the things of heaven, not the things of earth. For you died to this life, and your real life is hidden with Christ in God. And when Christ, who is your life, is revealed to the whole world, you will share in all his glory."

Colossians 3:1-4 AMP

"If then you have been raised with Christ [to a new life, this sharing His resurrection from the dead], aim at and seek the [rich, eternal treasures] that are above, where Christ is, seated at the right hand of God. And set your minds and keep Them set on what is above (the higher things), not on the things that are on the earth. For [as far as this world is concerned] you have died, and your [new, real] life is hidden with Christ in God. When Christ, Who is our life, appears, then you also will appear with Him in [the splendor of His] glory."

Interesting, isn't it? As Paul begins chapter 3, the first order of business he turned his attention to is the grand topic of Heaven. Contrary to the common opinion of many Christians today, who are consumed with what they would call *"practical Christianity"*, Paul is telling us that the number one priority for every Christian, in terms of our daily living, needs to be an understanding *about* Heaven, and a chasing *after* Heaven!

Heaven Should Be Our Priority?!?

The great apostle is boldly declaring that the Christian should be one who is living *like* Heaven, looking *towards* Heaven, and laboring *for* Heaven! He's telling us that every person who calls Jesus Christ their Lord and Master, should be making a "bee line" for the Kingdom of Heaven, in their hearts and minds!

So, let me ask you the obvious application question:

Does that describe your Christian life?

Is your walk with Jesus characterized by *a passion* for Heaven, *a longing* for His Kingdom, and *a serious laboring* to make heavenly investments for your future inheritance? Do you *consciously* go through your week *thinking* about Heaven? Could someone who knows you well accurately describe your relationship with the Lord as *"a person who regularly thinks about Heaven"*?

Sadly, I think that if we were honest, we'd admit that this simply isn't the case with most Christians... probably not even with ourselves! It seems that the average Christian believer, in today's fast-paced and busy society, just isn't in the habit of pausing and reflecting on such high and lofty topics like the Kingdom of Heaven. Most of us would probably say our lives are simply "too busy", and though we try to walk with the Lord, and think of Him as much as we can, we're simply not in the habit of contemplating eternity and Heaven in our daily lives.

One reason this is true, is that many of us have wrong concepts and unbiblical ideas about Heaven. For example, if your children were to ask you, *"Mommy and Daddy, what is Heaven like?"* Would you tell them the "Looney Tunes version" of Heaven? Maybe you'd say, *"Son, you're going to be on a cloud with wings sticking out of your back, strumming a harp forever."* Perhaps you'd answer *"Son, we're just going to be in Heaven, singing to the Lord, for ever and ever and ever, for all of eternity."* Though that is a common answer, I hope that's not what you would teach your kids. But if that is the case, then this book should be a great benefit to you and your family!

Paul the apostle clearly taught that Heaven should be the direction of life for all who've come to Jesus Christ for salvation. Recall his words to the Christians in Colossae:

"If then you were raised with Christ, seek those things which are above, where Christ is, sitting at the right hand of God. Set your mind on things above, not on things on the earth."
- Colossians 3:1 NKJV

Now some of you reading this book might be new Christians, and "young" in your faith. Others of you might not be new to Christianity, but would still consider yourselves "young" in terms of your under-standing of the subject of Heaven. If so, then this is a great time for you to be reading this book. Now you can do things the right way, and truly begin to focus on the first order of business in your walk with Jesus: *Living for Heaven for the rest of your life!*

This is to be our new direction–towards Heaven! Paul's first phrase in Colossians 3:1 is interesting, where he says:

"If then you were raised with Christ.."

Now what Paul is doing here, is referring us back to Colossians chapter 2. This is where Paul told us about the RADICAL transformation that took place in your heart when you accepted Christ, as Lord and Savior. Jesus shared the power of His resurrected life with you, and He transformed your heart and spirit when you became a Christian!

Radical Transformation From Christ!

Whether you're a new believer, whether you got saved last week, or whether you've been saved for 20 or 30 years, it doesn't matter. When Jesus came into your heart, you were radically changed on the inside! You were *"raised with Christ"* as Paul declared. Here's what he told the Colossians:

"In Him you were also circumcised with the circumcision made without hands, by putting off the body of the sins of the flesh, by the circumcision of Christ, buried with Him in baptism, in which you also were raised with Him

through faith in the working of God, who raised
Him from the dead. And you, being dead in your
trespasses and the uncircumcision of your flesh,
He has made alive together with Him, having
forgiven you all trespasses.."
– Colossians 2:11-13 NKJV

Paul is saying that when you became a Christian, Jesus came into your life and He spiritually *"cut away"* your sinful nature. You were *"circumcised"* spiritually by Christ Himself, and you were spiritually *"baptized"* into Jesus and His work for you upon the Cross. What this means is that you were united with Him in His death and resurrection. Just like Jesus rose up from the grave, you rose up to new life as well!

When you accepted Christ, the power of sin over your life was broken once and for all, and thru Christ living inside of you, you now have the ability to live a new and powerful "resurrection life" just like Jesus! Whether you believe this or not, or understand it fully or not, it's still true and can change your life if you live it out practically!

So, when you were born again by surrendering to Christ, a _radical transformation_ happened! Your sinful nature was cut away. You were _raised_ with Christ. He also told us in chapter 2, you received brand-new spiritual life. You were _regenerated_. Your dead spirit was given life by the Holy Spirit and you were brought to life. And lastly, Paul told us that you were _redeemed_. Paul put it like this:

"..having wiped out the handwriting of
requirements that was against us, which was

contrary to us. And He has taken it out of the way, having nailed it to the cross."
– Colossians 2:14 NKJV

This *"handwriting"* that is mentioned by Paul is the long list of sins that you had committed against the Lord, and deserved eternal punishment for. The Romans called this the *"titulus"* and this was the list that was nailed to the cross above a criminal, detailing the crimes he was guilty of. Remember, Jesus had a similar *"titulus"* placed above Him on the cross as well. We're told in Matthew 27:37 and Luke 23:38 that it was written in Hebrew, Latin, and Greek stating that He was *"Jesus of Nazareth, King of the Jews."*

Amazingly, Paul tells us that your *"titulus"*, the list of your cosmic crimes against God Almighty, was taken out of the way and nailed where? To the cross of Jesus Christ! The list of your sins was nailed to His cross...where He paid for them all, perfectly! (John 19:30)

As we said, this means that you were _radically transformed_ when you became a Christian. If you have NOT experienced radical transformation since you accepted Christ, then you might not know Jesus as your Savior. Because if you truly know Him, you'll have been _radically changed_ in your heart and spirit, and this transformation will show itself in your daily living.

I encourage you, take time to examine yourself and be sure that you have surrendered to Jesus, turned away from your sins, and asked Him to cleanse and save you by His sacrifice. (2 Corinthians 13:5; Matthew 7:16-23)

Paul is saying that since you have experienced radical transformation, *just like Jesus lived a new resurrection life* when he was risen from the dead, *so should you!* In other words, the things that *Jesus did* when He rose from the dead, *you should do too,* now that you're spiritually risen from the grave.

WDJD–What Did Jesus Do?

Remember a couple years ago when those WWJD bracelets were really popular? If you ever had one, it's actually a very good phrase: "WWJD–What Would Jesus Do?" But there's an even better phrase than WWJD? It's WDJD. Not "What *Would* Jesus Do?", but rather "What *Did* Jesus Do?"

Sometimes you just don't really know what Jesus would do in that same situation. You may not know for sure. But if you ask the question, "What *Did* Jesus Do?" it's an objective question, that we can easily answer. We can look into the pages of Scripture and see how Christ lived! So as we look at the Bible and ask this question "WDJD", what did Jesus actually do when He rose from the dead? Because whatever He did, you and I should copy. It's well been said, that instead of being a "copycats", Christians should really be "copy-Christs". In other words, if you're risen with Christ, live like Jesus lived after He physically rose from the dead, in new life!

#1–Jesus Left the Tomb

One of the first things Jesus did, was rise from the grave and walk out of the tomb He was buried in. *You should too!* If you're a Christian, a genuine follower of Christ, you should also leave the tomb behind, and never return to it! The place of death, darkness, and decomposition where you used to dwell, needs to be left behind for good! This will usually involve leaving friends. Leaving relationships. Leaving habits. Leaving places. You need to leave "dead" and sinful things behind and walk in a new and risen life, just like Jesus did, when He rose from the grave!

#2–Jesus Served Others

Jesus left the tomb, but He also spent time ministering to His disciples! For 40 days after Jesus rose from the dead, He was talking and teaching, serving and ministering, to those around Him–*so should you!*

Maybe you're new Christian and you don't know what to focus on. Well, there's two things you should prioritize: Number one, leave the tomb behind–the dead sinful things of your past. Number two, hang out with Christians and serve them just like Jesus! Your best friends, your closest relationships, your most intimate associations, need to be with the people of God. Should you have non-Christians as friends? Yes. You should pray for them, love them, and witness to them. But your closest friends, your buddies, and the people that you spend the most time with, should be the people of God.

As Jesus loved and served his disciples, you and I should be involved in loving and serving the people of God as well! Be sure to get involved in your local church and be active in giving back to the Christian family around you. They will love and serve you too, but as a "risen to new life" Christian, you should copy Jesus, by serving others!

#3–Jesus Moved in Supernatural Power

The third thing Jesus did after His Resurrection, was that He moved in supernatural power from the Holy Spirit. Jesus did things after He was risen from the dead, that were never done by Him before. His body functioned in a supernatural way, and He did amazing things which were not possible before. He moved with supernatural power and guess what–*so should you!* If you are truly risen with Christ, born again, and filled with the Holy Spirit, then *right now* you have the power to do things as a believer, that were impossible for you before!

Even if you just gave your life to Christ just a few days ago, as a Christian you now have the indwelling power of God's Holy Spirit to conquer sin, and say "NO!" to temptation. You have the power to love sacrificially like Jesus, *right now*. You have the power to be a faithful husband, *right now*. You have the power to be a good loving wife, an obedient son and daughter, *right now*. You have the power to live a supernaturally wholly Christ-centered life, *right now*, for the rest of your life! This is the revolutionary truth of what Paul is teaching the Colossians. If you are risen with Jesus Christ, then you have the power to live like Him, *right now! (Romans 6:1-18; Ephesians 5:18; Acts 1:8)*

#4–Jesus Lived for Heaven

However, there is one other thing that Jesus did after the Resurrection, that most of us don't realize: ***He lived for Heaven!*** He not only left the tomb, ministered to Christians, and moved in supernatural power. Jesus also looked forward to Heaven, and was focused on the Kingdom after rising from the grave – *and you should too!* Again, answer these simple questions:

> ***How many times a day do you***
> ***think about Heaven?***
> ***How many times per week do you imagine***
> ***the realities of the Kingdom?***

Most Christians I talk to, rarely ever think about Heaven during their workday. Very seldom does the average Christian allow the truth of Heaven to encourage, inspire, or empower them throughout their busy week. But the Lord doesn't want it to be like that for us! After His Resurrection, Jesus was *seeking* the things of Heaven, *speaking* of Heaven, and *anticipating* Heaven. Paul commanded us to do the same when he wrote:

> ***"If then you were raised with Christ,***
> ***seek those things which are above.."***
> ***– Colossians 3:1 NKJV***

Paul chose his words carefully, because this word ***"seek"*** is very powerful in the original Koine Greek language of the New Testament. This is the word ***"zéteó"*** which is a passionate, powerful, and aggressive word in the Greek . ***"Zéteó"*** means to strive after, to crave something, to desire, and to long for it. I envision a runner who's racing towards the finish line, pushing with everything he's got! You could also picture a person who is desperately reaching for a cup of water, because they're dying of thirst. It speaks of craving, longing, or seeking passionately for something. This is the word that Paul uses–**"zéteó"**.

Interestingly, the tense of the Greek verb, is in the *"present tense"*, it's in the *"active"*, and in the *"imperative"*. What does that mean? *"Present tense"* means you need to do this now. *"Active"* means you have to give effort and perform this action. The *"imperative"* means you must do this urgently!

It's as if Paul the apostle is saying *"Hey, right now, in the present moment, you must consciously choose to perform the action of striving after Heaven, and you must do this urgently, Christians!"* Wow! That puts a whole other spin his command to the Colossians to *"..seek the things which are above..."*

How do we know that Jesus was *passionately seeking* the things of Heaven? Let me share some verses that make this very obvious. In John 13, when Jesus was at the Last Supper, it tells us something interesting, which many of us overlook:

"Jesus, knowing that the Father had given all things into His hands,
and that He had come from God and was going to God.."
– John 13:3 NKJV

Jesus *knew* His direction was towards Heaven. He *knew* that after He was killed and resurrected, forty days later, He would ascend into Heaven and be with His Father. Jesus *knew* where He was going. This was

His focus. This was His conscious and willful intention. He spoke to His disciples about this in the next chapter, John 14, when they finally understood that He was going to die. They were scared. They were frightened. They were freaked out. That's when Jesus declared these famous words:

"Let not your heart be troubled; you believe in God, believe also in Me. In My Father's house are many mansions; if it were not so, I would have told you. I go to prepare a place for you. And if I go and prepare a place for you, I will come again and receive you to Myself; that where I am, there you may be also."
– John 14:1-3 NKJV

We can see that in this moment of fear and anxiety, Jesus' spiritual "antidepressant" was the hope of Heaven. It wasn't a pill. It wasn't some chemical injection. It was spiritual instruction about the coming Kingdom! The biblical cure for depression and anxiety... is Heaven!

The next time you or your spouse are sad or depressed, get out your Bible, spend time in the Word, and spiritually "inject" yourself with the hope of Heaven. This is exactly what Jesus did with His disciples! Across the pages of the Gospels, He frequently talked to his disciples about the reality of the Kingdom of Heaven.

As a matter of fact, Jesus had previously told his disciples the very same thing that Paul had taught the Colossians. Paul challenged his readers to, *"seek the things that are above."* However, in Matthew's Gospel, Jesus declared:

> **"Seek first the kingdom of God and his righteousness..."**
> **– Matthew 6:33 NKJV**

In this chapter of Matthew, Jesus was instructing to His disciples about unbelievers and non-Christians. Essentially, Jesus taught that the primary concerns of unbelievers are money, clothing, and material possessions. He said the unsaved man is focused on the physical, and temporary things of this life. It's a characteristic mark of non-Christians according to Christ.

May the Lord help us, as believers, to not be materialistic and primarily concerned about the passing things of this world! Jesus commands His disciples to not live in a way that is focused on the physical possessions and gathering financial riches. Rather, He tells us to *"seek"* as the first priority of our lives, the Kingdom of God.

The word **"seek"** that Jesus used here is exactly the same Greek word, **"zéteó"** that Paul chose. Jesus is teaching His disciples to *"seek, strive after, long for, desire earnestly"* the Kingdom of Heaven! It's as if He's saying *"Now, in the present moment, you must do this disciples–seek the Kingdom with all that you have! Make it the top concern and number one priority of your lives!"*

Jesus was clearly challenging them to passionately pursue after Heaven. He told them something similar to this earlier in the chapter. Jesus declared to the disciples:

"Do not lay up for yourselves treasures on earth, where moth and rust destroy and where thieves break in and steal; but lay up for yourselves treasures in heaven, where neither moth nor rust destroys and where thieves do not break in and steal. For where your treasure is, there your heart will be also."
– Matthew 6:19-21 NKJV

In modern day language, Jesus is telling us to make a kind of *"Heavenly 401(k)"* by investing our time, energy, and financial resources into expanding the Kingdom of God. Amazing! In other words, when we serve Him, when we tithe, anything we do for the Lord out of a heart motivated by love, Jesus is telling us that we are storing it up as treasure in Heaven! Unfortunately, we have a hard time believing that. Many Christians today say things like *"Oh, come on. Let's be practical. That sounds a bit strange. Let's keep our feet on the ground!"*

CS Lewis, a great Christian author, commented on this type of disbelief in his book *"The Problem of Pain."* In his days, it seems that many people were primarily concerned with simply improving this temporary world, and not bothering about the next one. CS Lewis said this:

"We are very shy nowadays of even mentioning Heaven. We are afraid of the jeer, being made fun of, about the pie-in-the-sky. And of being

told that we are trying to escape from the duty of making a happy world here and now and making dreams of a happy world elsewhere. But either there is pie-in-the-sky, Heaven, or there is not, if there is not, then Christianity is false. Because this doctrine is woven into its whole fabric. But if there is, then this truth like any other, must be faced whether you think it's useful or not."

CS Lewis was absolutely right. Today we're also very shy of mentioning the truth of Heaven. I talk to many Christians, who just like the people in Lewis' day, are primarily focused on the things of this life. They say *"Come on! I have to pay my electric bill. I have to focus on my income, my house, my car. I don't have time to think about "pie in the sky!" Be practical!"* Many Christians have even told me: *"Listen, be careful about all this talk and teaching of Heaven. You might be so "heavenly minded" that you'll be no earthly good!"*

Have you heard things like that before? Or perhaps have you've even been the one who's said that to others? I sure hope not–because that perspective is completely unbiblical! The scriptural position is essentially this: *"You cannot be of any true earthly good, until you are heavenly minded!"* CS Lewis agreed with this, and commented on it in his book, "Mere Christianity" where he wrote:

"If you read history, you will find the Christians who did the most for the present world were just those who thought the most of the next. It

*is since Christians have largely ceased to think
of the other world, that they have become so
ineffective in this one."*

I wholeheartedly agree with Lewis! You see,
Christians used to talk about Heaven a lot more that
we do today. Two hundred years ago, Heaven was
called the "North Star" of the Christian church by
many. Centuries ago, captains would navigate their
ships at night time by looking at the North Star. This
heavenly beacon in the night sky would guide them
through the stormy waters of the ocean, to arrive
safely at their destination. So, in the same way, the
Christian church is to be guided through the storms
of this life, by focusing on the reality of Heaven!

This world can be hard and rough, at times. Often,
we feel as though we're in stormy waters and have
lost our way. We're persecuted. We're chased. We're
hunted. But Jesus wants us to know and remember
this: *Heaven is coming!* If we choose to look thru
the fog of this life, and keep our minds fixed on this
beautiful truth, we'll be able to navigate the stormy
seas of life so much better!

The book Revelation, which speaks so much
about Heaven, was written in the year 96A.D. by the
Apostle John, on the prison island of Patmos. What
most people are unaware of, is that Revelation was
given to Christians who were being brutally persecuted, and systematically hunted by the Roman government. They would often stand in the Coliseum,
with the Caesar looking down upon them from the
podium, signaling for their death. Gladiators would
then surround them with weapons of execution, or

wild beasts would be released upon them to devour their flesh!

What could they think of to strengthen them in their hour of need? Where could they anchor their souls for spiritual strength? They could find power and courage through the reality of Heaven! They could say *"Lord, I'm about to die for you, but that's okay. Very soon, the situation will be reversed. You will conquer this world in glory and power, you will set things right, and your disciples will rule and reign at your side forever!"* Such was the case for tens of thousands of believers who were martyred for their faith. The hope of Heaven was given to them for strength and power in their hour of need, while facing death!

A Pastor is Burned Alive!

In the second century A.D., the pastor of the church in Smyrna, named Polycarp, was killed for his faith. The historical account of his death shows us the power that the truth of Heaven gives to the heart of a believer, as he faced the fires of martyrdom in 156A.D.:

As Polycarp was being taken into the arena, a voice came to him from heaven: "Be strong, Polycarp and play the man!" No one saw who had spoken, but our brothers who were there heard the voice. When the crowd heard that Polycarp had been captured, there was an uproar.

The Proconsul asked him whether he was Polycarp. On hearing that he was, he tried to persuade him to apostatize, saying, "Have respect for your old age, swear by the fortune of Caesar. Repent, and say, 'Down with the Atheists!'"

Polycarp looked grimly at the wicked heathen multitude in the stadium, and gesturing towards them, he said, "Down with the Atheists!"

"Swear," urged the Proconsul, "reproach Christ, and I will set you free."

"86 years I have served him," Polycarp declared, "and he has done me no wrong. How can I blaspheme my King and my Savior?"

"I have wild animals here," the Proconsul said. "I will throw you to them if you do not repent."

"Call them," Polycarp replied. "It is unthinkable for me to repent from what is good to turn to what is evil. I will be glad though to be changed from evil to righteousness."

"If you despise the animals, I will have you burned."

"You threaten me with fire which burns for an hour, and is then extinguished, but you know nothing of the fire of the coming judgment and eternal punishment, reserved for the ungodly. Why are you waiting? Bring on whatever you want."

It was all done in the time it takes to tell. The crowd collected wood and bundles of sticks from the shops and public baths. When the pile was ready, they went to fix him with nails, he said, "Leave me as I am, for He that gives me strength to endure the fire, will enable me not to struggle, without the help of your nails." So they simply tied him with his hands behind him, like a ram chosen for sacrifice.

He was then burned alive and pierced with a sword until dead. This is the story of the blessed Polycarp, the pastor and twelfth martyr in Smyrna.

You see, Heaven was the North Star, which empowered the Early Church, strengthened the historical Church, but has been largely forgotten by the "Modern Church." This is a shame. It was a major topic in pulpits 200 years ago, but today is rarely (if ever) taught upon. However, CS Lewis is right. If you read history, you will find that Christians who did the most for the present world, were those who thought the most of the next!

Maybe at this point you're thinking something like this:

"Ahhh, we can't really know what Heaven is going to be like. The Bible doesn't exactly tell us, and we can't really be sure. Besides, Paul told us that 'Eye has not seen, nor ear heard, Nor have entered into the heart of man The things which God has prepared for those who love Him.'"

Have you ever quoted that verse about Heaven? Can I tell you a secret? That verse from 1 Corinthians 2:9 has absolutely *nothing* to do with Heaven! But it's probably the most often quoted verse I ever hear from Christians on this topic. However, if you examine what Paul is speaking about, he's actually contrasting the wisdom of God and the wisdom of man. He is teaching how the people of this world, it's rulers, and demons cannot understand or perceive the plan of God in history. But, in the very next verse, Paul says that the Lord has indeed revealed them to us, His children! Please don't make the mistake of thinking that Paul meant you can't understand the doctrine of Heaven – that was the furthest thing from his mind!

How Many Chapters About Heaven?!?

Did you know the Bible says A LOT about Heaven? It's a topic that the Lord has devoted a large amount of scripture to in the Bible. Would you like to guess how many chapters, Old and New Testament, deal with this amazing doctrine of Heaven? Not just 10, not just 20, or 50, or even a hundred...there are about 110 chapters in the Bible that I've found, teaching us details and specific information about Heaven. One hundred and ten chapters – wow! Yes, you can know what Heaven will be like, to a very large degree! If the Holy Spirit has inspired 110 chapters on this topic, it's obvious to see that this is an important truth to God. He wants it to be important to you, too!

Like Polycarp, when your time comes, and you are close to the doorway of death, what will be your hope in those dark hours? Heaven! Why? Because you'll be able to paint a full-color three-dimensional picture of it in your minds, fueled by the 110 chapters of the Bible that speak of it. God wants to fuel the fires of your imagination, using the Scriptures, and enable you to "see" your eternal home with eyes of faith, giving you power for your present, and hope for your future!

Adam Clarke, the Bible commentator from the 1700s, had this to say regarding Heaven:

> *"We should love heavenly things.*
> *We should study them.*
> *You should let your hearts be entirely*
> *engrossed by them!"*

I couldn't agree more with this old preacher! We should *LOVE* the things of Heaven. We should *yearn* and *thirst* and *long* for Heaven. Adam Clarke said we should study them. In other words, after we discover the chapters in the Bible that deal with the topic of Heaven, we should study them in detail. We ought to think about them often, discuss them frequently, and study diligently the things of the Kingdom! This is how Heaven will become one of the major passions of your life, and empower your walk with Jesus. In this book we aim to help you do exactly that!

However, we still have a big problem. Most of us as Christians can't truly *"seek"*, or *"zéteó"*, the things of Heaven, as Paul commanded. Most of us cannot *"set our minds"* on the things of Heaven correctly yet. Why not? Because we don't really understand Heaven biblically. Most Christians have a big confusion here, and therefore, a hard time in living for Heaven practically. In this book, our goal is to correct that condition!

In order for you to *"seek"* after Heaven, and to *"set our minds"* on the Kingdom, we're now going to dive head first into this beautiful doctrine of Heaven. We're going to examine multiple chapters about it in Scripture, and see what the Lord has revealed about our glorious and eternal destiny in the Kingdom of God. The goal will be, that after you're finished reading this book, you'll know exactly what you're supposed to *"seek"* after, and how to pursue it practically in your life. We're going to do what Adam Clarke said, and let our minds be engrossed by the things of Heaven! Here we go!

An Important **PHRASE** About Heaven

I want to start by teaching you an important and helpful *phrase* about Heaven. Slogans and sayings can be very powerful and helpful in our learning, as effective memory devices. So here is a profoundly simple and a simply profound phrase for your understanding of Heaven. Here it is:

"Heaven is coming to earth!"

If you understand this simple phrase, and all that is contained within it, you'll be miles ahead of most Christians. The Scriptures clearly teach us that ultimately, Heaven is coming down to earth, and God's Kingdom will physically be established over the entire planet. If we really understand this idea, what does it teach us about Heaven?

#1 – Heaven is/will be a real, literal place

This is very basic, but it's news to many Christians. There will be a real location and geography to Heaven. It will contain cities, lakes, trees, nations, people, animals, etc…because it is *real* and it's coming to a *real* location – our very own planet earth!

So when you find yourself envisioning Heaven (which I hope you begin to do!), you should picture it very similar to how the earth looks now. It will have mountains, towns, culture, different occupations, a variety of countries, etc.. – just like planet earth does in the present. When the Kingdom of Heaven comes to earth, it will be much more like our present experience than most people realize!

However, the major difference will be the absence of sin and evil. In the beginning of the 1,000 year Kingdom called the "Millennium", sin will still be present in some humans, will be minutely monitored, and swiftly punished with "iron clad" justice on the earth. It won't be practiced by the saints, as we'll have perfected, sinless, glorified, resurrection bodies. However, those humans who survive the Tribulation and are allowed entrance into the Kingdom, will still possess the capacity to sin. Eventually, in the New Heavens and New Earth, all sin everywhere will be removed and eradicated. In this final stage of God's plan, the world will truly be perfect and sinless as we all long for it to be, and as the Lord has promised it to be!

Just imagine: A world that is totally purified, perfectly holy, and under the complete control of Jesus. You and your saved family will be there, in powerful resurrection bodies, serving the Lord on a New

Earth. That is what Heaven will look like, according to the Scriptures!

#2 – Heaven is/will be a real, physical experience

Where is it coming to? To earth! It's not going to be on a cloud somewhere. You won't be strumming a harp for all eternity (as Looney Tunes would have you believe). That's what I call "Cartoon Christianity". The concept of eternity on a cloud with a harp wouldn't be Heaven at all…especially for those of us who aren't musically inclined!

That's *not* what Heaven will be like! Many people make the mistake of thinking that they will be some sort of spirit, ghost, or angelic type of creature in Heaven. According to the Bible, this is absolutely false. Adam was created with a perfect physical body in Genesis 1, in order to enjoy a perfect physical earth that the Lord gave to him. Similarly, in Revelation 22 the redeemed will again be walking on a perfect (and remade) earth, in perfect, resurrected, and glorified bodies. That's what Heaven will be like!

Though it will be different that your life now, in many ways, it will also be very similar. We were created with bodies to experience the physical world around us, and this earth was graciously created by the Lord for man to enjoy! A physical planet earth will become the new "capital planet" in a remade universe in the New Heavens and New Earth, ultimately! That's what Heaven *will* be like!

The 3 Major **PHASES** Of Heaven

Now, that we've learned the important *phrase* concerning Heaven, we're going to teach you the 3 major *phases* of Heaven. I truly believe that if you can memorize these 3 simple phases of God's Eternal Plan, it will greatly help you to understand and remember the doctrine of Heaven, easily and effectively!

The Divine Trinity:

In Christianity as you've may have noticed, we have many "trinities". **First, of course we have GOD, the Divine Trinity.** This is the truth that we worship the one true GOD, Who exists in three separate and distinct holy Persons: God, the Father; God, the Son; God, the Holy Spirit. The truth of the Trinity is undeniably taught in both the Old and New Testaments, and is one of the "cornerstones" of the historical Christian faith. *(See Gen 1:1 "Elohim"; Gen 1:26; Num 6:24-26; Isa 6:3, 48:16, 63:3-8; John 1:1-3; Matt 3:16-17, 28:18-20; 2Cor 13:14; Rev 1:4-5)*

The Human "Trinity":

You, as a human, are also a kind of "trinity." You are one person and yet you exist in 3 unique parts: body, soul, and spirit. Paul mentions this in 1 Thessalonians 5:23, that the Lord would sanctify the saints in their "body, soul, and spirit." Your body is the physical part of you; your soul (Greek "psyche") is the mind, will, and emotions; and your spirit is the part of you that fellowships with your Creator, once you're born again thru Jesus Christ.

The Gospel "Trinity":

The Gospel is a kind of "trinity" as well. Contrary to common practice, telling someone *"Jesus loves you!"* is not sharing the Gospel (though it's a great thing to do!). As we read 1 Corinthians 15 and Romans 10 we see that there are 3 essential elements to the biblical Gospel or "Good News" of salvation: *1) Jesus is God. 2) Jesus died for sin. 3) Jesus rose for sin.* This is the New Testament Gospel. It's vital to share these 3 truths, as we witness to our friends and family about Christ.

The "Trinity" of Heaven:

Heaven is one doctrine, but has 3 separate phases. Again, I truly believe that if you can memorize these 3 simple phases of God's Eternal Plan, it will help you understand the doctrine of Heaven very effectively! The 3 phases are easy to remember:

Phase #1 – The *Dimension* of Heaven
Phase #2 – The *Kingdom* of Heaven
Phase #3 – The *Eternal* Heavens

If you can memorize these 3 *phases* of Heaven, along with the *phrase* ("Heaven is coming to the earth!") you'll be further ahead in your understanding of the doctrine of Heaven, than about 95% of Christians. Let me briefly describe them, before we examine each phase in depth:

"**The Dimension of Heaven**" is the first phase of Heaven unfolding for us. Today, when a Christian dies, this is where their spirit will go – to this other "realm" or "dimension" called Heaven. If you walked outside today and died, when you "opened your eyes" in eternity, this Dimension of Heaven is what you would see. This is why theologians call it the "Present Heaven", because this is where believers presently go when they die. When John looked into the Throne Room of Heaven (Rev 4,5) this is what he was looking at. When Isaiah got a sneak-peek into the heavenly realm, this is what the Lord showed him. We'll be examining this exciting phase of Heaven in the next chapter.

"**The Kingdom of Heaven**" comes next in the unfolding of God's eternal plan. This is the thousand-year rule of Jesus Christ upon the earth. It's also called the "Millennium", from the Latin phrase *"mille anum"* or a thousand years (Rev 20:1-6). This phase comes when Jesus returns to earth in the Second Coming, and rules and reigns over all the earth for a thousand years. This "Golden Age" of God upon the earth, spoken of in great volume by the prophets of the Old Testament, is the long awaited Kingdom of Heaven. At the end of this phase, the Great White Throne Judgement will take place, in which all the unrighteous dead will be condemned and cast into the Lake of Fire (Rev 20:7-15). We'll examine this in chapter 3 of this book.

"**The Eternal Heavens**" is the final and ultimate phase of Heaven. This is when the universe is finally refashioned by GOD Himself, completely renewed, and totally perfected. This is when there will finally be no more death, pain, sickness, or sin. All of these aspects of the Fall of Adam and the resulting curse will finally be eradicated, and the entire universe will be made right once again! Earth will become the capital planet of a refashioned cosmos, under the perfect rule and reign of the Father, Son, and Spirit for all eternity, time without end! It is the ultimate "Happy Ending" to the spiritual drama of man's sinful rebellion, and God's amazing grace that relentlessly pursues us. We will rule and reign at the side of the LORD in the New Heavens and New Earth.. forever and ever! This will be our focus in chapter 4.

Now that you've had an introduction to the great topic of Heaven, and the importance of it in the Scriptures; now that you've gotten a short overview of the 3 phases that will unfold in God's plan of Heaven, I think it's time for us to dig into each of them individually and in greater detail. Let's begin now to examine each of these 3 phases of Heaven, and see what it will look like as God's eternal plan unfolds for humanity! Here we go....

Chapter 2

Phase #1: The Dimension of Heaven

This is the first phase that people will experience in the unfolding of God's plan. Now, if you want a keyword, a single idea that helps describe and summarize the "Dimension of Heaven", you should commit the word *"adoration"* to memory. Adoration, or worship, is the central concept that describes this first phase of Heaven, since it's one of the primary activities that'll be happening there.

<u>When Will We Arrive In Heaven?</u>

Understanding this phase, helps to answer certain questions we often have concerning death and our passing into the next world, such as:

"Where will Christians go when they die?"
"When a Christian opens their eyes in Heaven, what will they see?"
"Who will we be able to meet when we arrive in Heaven?"

Today, at the point of death, this is where the spirit of a Christian will immediately go to, the Dimension of Heaven. When you "open your eyes" after you die (or are Raptured), you will immediately find yourself standing in the Throne Room of GOD, surrounded by billions of angels, and all the redeemed believers of the ages. Since you're going to show up here someday, it would benefit you to pay attention to the details of this place, understanding what it is, and where things are. This way, when you show up, you won't be like a lost tourist in Heaven, but rather like a Heavenly "tour guide", knowing where everything is, and able to orient the new arrivals around you!

<u>What Does The Dimension Of Heaven Look Like?</u>

This first phase of Heaven is spoken about in both the Old and New Testaments. There are at least 7 whole chapters that teach us important truths about the Dimension of Heaven. Each of these chapters are like "snapshots" into the spiritual dimension, this other realm, this place where angels, the spirits of the redeemed, and God Himself dwells. Some notable chapters to examine on the Dimension of Heaven would be the following:

- **Revelation 4 & 5**
- **Ezekiel 1 & 10**
- **Isaiah 6**
- **Job 1 & 2**
- **1 Kings 22:19-23**

Let's examine Revelation chapter 4, and see what we can learn. It's certainly one of the best known chapters in the Bible describing the Dimension of Heaven, and it can teach us many of the primary features that you'll see when you arrive there. John the apostle, who wrote the book of Revelation, describes for us the Dimension of Heaven in his amazing vision that God gave him:

"After these things I looked, and behold, a door standing open in heaven. And the first voice which I heard was like a trumpet speaking with me, saying, "Come up here, and I will show you things which must take place after this." Immediately I was in the Spirit; and behold, a throne set in heaven, and One sat on the throne. And He who sat there was like a jasper and a sardius stone in appearance; and there was a rainbow around the throne, in appearance like an emerald. Around the throne were twenty-four thrones, and on the thrones I saw twenty-four elders sitting, clothed in white robes; and they had crowns of gold on their heads. And from the throne proceeded lightnings, thunderings, and voices. Seven lamps of fire were burning before the throne, which are the seven Spirits of God. Before the throne there was a sea of glass, like crystal. And in the midst of the throne, and around the throne, were four living creatures full of eyes in front and in back. The first living creature was like a lion, the second living creature like a calf, the third living creature had a face like a man, and the

fourth living creature was like a flying eagle. The four living creatures, each having six wings, were full of eyes around and within. And they do not rest day or night, saying: "Holy, holy, holy, Lord God Almighty, Who was and is and is to come!" Whenever the living creatures give glory and honor and thanks to Him who sits on the throne, who lives forever and ever, the twenty-four elders fall down before Him who sits on the throne and worship Him who lives forever and ever, and cast their crowns before the throne, saying: "You are worthy, O Lord, To receive glory and honor and power; For You created all things, And by Your will they exist and were created."
- Revelation 4:1-11 NKJV

The Throne Room Of GOD Almighty!

This breathtaking, and slightly mysterious envi-ronment, is what you can expect to see when you open your eyes in this Dimension of Heaven. As I said earlier, many theologians call this the "Present Heaven" because if you die presently, this is where you will go. When Paul says to be absent from the body is to be present with the Lord (2 Corinthians 5:1-9), this is the place he was referring to.

Upon arrival, the first thing that would catch your attention is the Throne, and the magnificent One seated upon it. You would immediately be aware that you are in the visible presence of the GOD of the universe – your personal Creator Himself! Notice in these verses that John makes reference to all 3 Persons of the Trinity. He sees God the Father upon the Throne, God the Spirit around the Throne (the seven lamps as in Isa 11:2), and God the Son standing before the Throne (Rev 5:1-14). He described it with these words:

"Immediately I was in the Spirit; and behold, a throne set in heaven, and One sat on the throne. And He who sat there was like a jasper and a sardius stone in appearance; and there was a rainbow around the throne... Seven lamps of fire were burning before the throne, which are the seven Spirits of God...

And I looked, and behold, in the midst of the throne and of the four living creatures, and in the midst of the elders, stood a Lamb as though it had been slain..."
– Revelation 4:2,3,5; 5:6 NKJV

The 3 Persons of the Trinity are the main focus and central feature of the Dimension of Heaven. Though other things may catch your gaze when you arrive, the Triune GOD Himself will command all your attention! As seen in the end of this chapter, being in the physical presence of GOD Almighty, will powerfully move you to worship Him and throw any crown you have at the feet of your great Father, King, and Creator! Adoration and worship will be the consuming passion of your heart, as you join with the chorus of innumerable angels, billions of redeemed believers of the ages, as you praise the very One who has eternally *loved* you, skillfully *created* you, graciously *redeemed* you, and ultimately *brought* you into the breathtaking Dimension of Heaven!

Who Will We See In The Dimension Of Heaven?

All the Christians, the saints of the ages, combined with the angelic armies of God, will be there, transfixed in awe before the Throne of GOD! As is obvious in this chapter, we will all be worshiping and praising the Lord as never before. Imagine the exhilaration of seeing the Lord with your own eyes, hearing billions of angelic warriors praising their Commander, and standing in the midst of believers such as David, Elijah, and Moses, as you all sing worshipfully to the Lord God together! Amazing!

John even describes one of the heavenly songs that will echo from the mouths of the redeemed saints:

"And they sang a new song, saying: "You are worthy to take the scroll, and to open its seals; For You were slain, and have redeemed us to God by Your blood out of every tribe and tongue and people and nation, and have made us kings and priests to our God; And we shall reign on the earth... saying with a loud voice: "Worthy is the Lamb who was slain to receive power and riches and wisdom, and strength and honor and glory and blessing!"
– Revelation 5:9-10,12 NKJV

If you want to be an overachiever in the heavenly scene, I'd suggest memorizing the lyrics of these worship songs (Rev 4:8-11; 5:9-14). That way you can teach them to other (less prepared) believers, as we praise the One seated upon the Throne! This is what you'll see upon arrival in the Dimension of Heaven. It's going to be glorious and completely awesome! The intimacy you will have with Christ in this moment will be unparalleled. This amazing worship experience will simply be mind-boggling, and wonderfully fulfilling in every part of your being!

Will Christians Receive Rewards In Heaven?

Another fascinating experience we'll have in this Dimension of Heaven, is being personally rewarded by Christ, for all of your faithful service and labor in His Kingdom. This is why John sees the Church casting their "crowns" or rewards before the Lord in worshipful adoration:

"Around the throne were twenty-four thrones, and on the thrones I saw twenty-four elders sitting, clothed in white robes; and they had crowns of gold on their heads... the twenty-four elders fall down before Him who sits on the throne and worship Him who lives forever and ever, and cast their crowns before the throne, saying: "You are worthy, O Lord, to receive glory and honor and power; For You created all things, and by Your will they exist and were created."
- Revelation 4:4, 10-11 NKJV

This is a very misunderstood, and even neglected truth by many Christians, and even pastors today. It appears that the most important moment for you as a Christian, will be when you stand before Jesus, in the Dimension of Heaven. This is when you will be rewarded and compensated, for all of your faithful service and sacrifice to your King, while upon the earth. This will be your meeting with your Master, and your interview with Immanuel!

This fateful day, called the "Judgement Seat of Christ" or the "Bema Seat Judgement", was of primary concern to Paul the apostle. He is the main source we have in the New Testament, for studying this momentous heavenly event. In 2 Corinthians Paul mentions the reality of this climactic day, when he writes:

"Therefore we make it our aim, whether present or absent, to be well pleasing to Him. For we must all appear before the judgment seat of Christ, that each one may receive the things done in the body, according to what he has done, whether good or bad."
– 2 Corinthians 5:9-10 NKJV

Obviously, this is a unique and special moment in the life of every believer. Paul says that each of us "must appear before the Judgement Seat of Christ" and that the purpose of this judgement, is to receive something from the Lord for how we served Him.

However, we're still left with questions, since Paul doesn't give us many details. The reason for this, is that in a previous letter, Paul had already given the Corinthians a detailed description of what this "Awards Ceremony" for the Christian will look like, and what we will experience. This is how Paul put it:

"... I have laid the foundation, and another builds on it. But let each one take heed how he builds on it. For no other foundation can anyone lay

than that which is laid, which is Jesus Christ.
Now if anyone builds on this foundation with
gold, silver, precious stones, wood, hay, straw,
each one's work will become clear; for the Day
will declare it, because it will be revealed by fire;
and the fire will test each one's work, of what
sort it is. If anyone's work which he has built on
it endures, he will receive a reward. If anyone's
work is burned, he will suffer loss;
but he himself will be saved, yet so as
through fire."
– 1 Corinthians 3:10-15 NKJV

From this information, we can derive a pretty clear picture of what will happen on the wonderful day when you are rewarded by your great King. Apparently, all that you've ever done for the Lord will be represented there in some visible form, since Paul pictures it here as different kinds of building materials (gold, silver, gems, wood, hay, straw). Interestingly, he likens the Christian life to a spiritual "building project" in which Christ is the great Foundation. Paul declares that everything we do for the Lord is either a good or poor kind of building material in constructing your "spiritual house" in the Lord.

What Will Christians Be Rewarded For?

First, we need to realize that Jesus *never* forgets even the smallest act of service or labor that you do for His Kingdom. We know this from the fact that Christ is God, and so knows *all* things (Psalm 139:1-6) and it's impossible for Him to forget *anything* (Malachi 3:6). But we also know this from specific things that

Jesus taught us concerning the faithful service of His disciples. For example, He declared that even giving a cup of cold water to a believer, in the love of Jesus, would be rewarded by Him:

**"And whoever gives one of these little ones only
a cup of cold water in the name of a disciple,
assuredly, I say to you, he shall by no means
lose his reward."
– Matthew 10:42 NKJV**

What?!? Jesus promises to reward us for simply giving a cold cup of water to another Christian? Yes! Every single act or service and of labor of love that you perform for Jesus, will be graciously rewarded by Him! Nothing you do for Christ is <u>ever</u> forgotten, and no act of service is <u>ever</u> in vain! (Read 1 Corinthians 15:58)

One day, Peter the apostle was curious about this issue of serving the Lord, and if He would ever reward them. Peter then posed a bold question to Jesus:

**"See, we have left all and followed You. Therefore,
what shall we have?" So Jesus said to them,
"Assuredly I say to you, that in the regeneration,
when the Son of Man sits on the throne of His
glory, you who have followed Me will also sit
on twelve thrones, judging the twelve tribes
of Israel. "And everyone who has left houses or
brothers or sisters or father or mother or wife
or children or lands, for My name's sake, shall**

receive a hundredfold, and inherit eternal life."
– Matthew 19:27-29 NKJV

It's clear to see from these and other verses, that the Lord takes our service to Him very seriously. Though most Christians are unaware or ignorant of our Master's heart on this issue, Jesus promises to faithfully and greatly reward His servants for their diligent labor in His Kingdom. After all, a great King and a just Master <u>must</u> compensate His workers for the service they give Him. (Luke 10:7; 1 Timothy 5:18)

How Will Rewards Be Decided By Jesus?
We now know that the Lord can never, and does never forget all you've done for Him. But the question remains, how exactly will these rewards and crowns be given out? At the Judgement Seat of Christ, how will the Lord determine what <u>you</u> receive on this amazing day? Look again at what Paul told us:

"...it will be revealed by fire; and the fire will test
each one's work, of what sort it is. If anyone's
work which he has built on it endures, he will
receive a reward. If anyone's work is burned, he
will suffer loss; but he himself will be saved,
yet so as through fire."
– 1 Corinthians 3:13-15 NKJV

Apparently, all that you've done for the Lord in your service will be represented before the Throne. A type of "fire" will pass through it and burn away the parts that aren't "fire-proof", represented by "wood, hay, straw." These parts that will "burn" away, are the aspects of your service to Jesus that were done with the wrong motivation. These are the moments of ministry, or the aspects of your serving His people, that weren't done with the proper motivation of love.

We know that the Lord sees and knows all, but He primarily look at our *hearts*, our internal motivations, at *why* we are doing things for Him and others. The Lord declared this principle to the prophet Samuel:

> **"Do not look at his appearance ...the LORD does not see as man sees; for man looks at the outward appearance, but the LORD looks at the heart."**
> **– 1 Samuel 16:7 NKJV**

This principle is true throughout all of our lives, but especially in this area of serving the Lord and others with a heart of *love*. After all, Jesus told us that the two greatest commandments for any human are to *love* the Lord and to *love* our neighbors, in all that we do (Matthew 22:35-40). Paul taught us that if we serve the Lord, and use our spiritual gifts in a way that isn't loving, it's essentially *worthless* in the eyes of God. He explained it like this:

> **"Though I speak with the tongues of men and of angels, but have not love, I have become sounding brass or a clanging cymbal. And though I have the gift of prophecy, and understand all mysteries and all knowledge, and though I have all faith, so that I could remove**

***mountains, but have not love, I am nothing. And
though I bestow all my goods to feed the poor,
and though I give my body to be burned, but
have not love, it profits me nothing."
– 1 Corinthians 13:1-3 NKJV***

This will be the standard Jesus uses as He evaluates Christians for their rewards and crowns at the Judgement Seat of Christ. The things that were not done with the motivation of _love_ for the Lord and people, will be burned away and lost.

However, what was done out of a pure motivation, and a heart of _love_, will endure the fire of Jesus' examination, be fashioned into a crown, and placed upon the head of the believer! What a glorious day that is coming!

Are "Crowns" In Heaven Important?

Some Christians are of the opinion that these crowns are just a minor issue and not very important. They say *"Who needs Crowns in Heaven? That doesn't really matter. I just want to make it there period!"* Unfortunately, although this attitude is prevalent among Christians, it couldn't be further from the truth!

Jesus taught about heavenly rewards more than most people ever realize. We've already seen that He promised to compensate His servants for even the smallest acts of kindness, such as giving a cup of water in love. We learned that Jesus greatly rewards those people who, like the apostles, lay down their lives in sacrificial service to Him and His Kingdom. As a matter of fact, did you know that one of the last things Jesus said, in the entire Bible, focuses on rewarding His faithful servants? He declared this, in the last chapter of Revelation:

> *"And behold, I am coming quickly, and My reward is with Me, to give to every one according to his work."*
> *– Revelation 22:12 NKJV*

Obviously, this is very important in the mind and heart of our Lord, as He chose to mention it in the closing chapter of the entire Bible. Though many Christians believe it's not important, Jesus would highly disagree!

During His earthly ministry, Jesus gave frequent teachings about His heavenly "Rewards Program". These teachings help us understand the _great_ importance that the Judgement Seat of Christ should occupy in our hearts, as we seek to serve the Lord faithfully in the present. Jesus put it like this, in what we commonly call the "Parable of the Minas" in Luke's Gospel:

> *"Now as they heard these things, He spoke another parable, because He was near Jerusalem and because they thought the kingdom of God would appear immediately. Therefore, He said: "A certain nobleman went into a far country to receive for himself a kingdom and to return. "So he called ten of his servants, delivered to them ten minas, and said to them, 'Do business till I come.' "But his citizens hated him, and sent a delegation after him, saying, 'We will not have*

this man to reign over us.' "And so it was that when he returned, having received the kingdom, he then commanded these servants, to whom he had given the money, to be called to him, that he might know how much every man had gained by trading. "Then came the first, saying, 'Master, your mina has earned ten minas.' "And he said to him, 'Well done, good servant; because you were faithful in a very little, have authority over ten cities.' "And the second came, saying, 'Master, your mina has earned five minas.' "Likewise he said to him, 'You also be over five cities.' "Then another came, saying, 'Master, here is your mina, which I have kept put away in a handkerchief. 'For I feared you, because you are an austere man. You collect what you did not deposit, and reap what you did not sow.' "And he said to him, 'Out of your own mouth I will judge you, you wicked servant. You knew that I was an austere man, collecting what I did not deposit and reaping what I did not sow. 'Why then did you not put my money in the bank, that at my coming I might have collected it with interest?' "And he said to those who stood by, 'Take the mina from him, and give it to him who has ten minas.' ("But they said to him, 'Master, he has ten minas.') 'For I say to you, that to everyone who has will be given; and from him who does not have, even what he has will be taken away from him. 'But bring here those enemies of mine, who did not want me to reign over them, and slay them before me.' "
– Luke 19:11-27 NKJV

<u>We learn at least 4 things from this well-known teaching of Jesus:</u>

1) He's given resources **to every one of us,** to use and invest for His Kingdom.
2 He expects us to **be faithful and diligent** in using these gifts and talents.
3) He wants us to **expand His Kingdom,** as we wait for Heaven to come.
4) He will **greatly reward His disciples,** who serve their King faithfully!

You see, this is one of the reasons why the Judgement Seat of Christ is the most important day, of the rest of your eternity: *It will determine <u>who</u> you are, and <u>what</u> you do in the Kingdom of Heaven...<u>forever</u>!* If that's not important to you, then I don't really know what is! This is why Jesus and the apostles talked so much about the "Doctrine of Rewards" in the coming Kingdom – it will decide the actual quality of your personal eternity!

The word for *"crown"* that is used in Revelation 4 and in the rest of the New Testament, is the Greek word **"stephanos"** meaning a wreath or garland that was given to the winners of the Olympic Games in Greece. It was also given to victorious soldiers by their military commander, after a great battle was won.

These *"crowns"* will also be used to honor and recognize the faithful servants of Jesus in the Dimension of Heaven. Our King and Commander will choose to reward His loyal and sacrificial soldiers, with this greatest of all "battlefield decorations" as they stand before His Throne in Heaven. Just as the Olympic judges of Greece would recognize the victorious athletes for their exertion, sweat, and labor, so the Judge of Heaven will reward faithful Christians who have completed the "race of faith" and made it to the finish line!

These crowns will determine _who_ you are and _what_ you do in the Kingdom of Heaven. We can see this very clearly in Jesus' words:

"Then came the first, saying, 'Master, your mina has earned ten minas.' "And he said to him, 'Well done, good servant; because you were faithful in a very little, have authority over ten cities.' "And the second came, saying, 'Master, your mina has earned five minas.' "Likewise he said to him, 'You also be over five cities.'
– Luke 19:16-19 NKJV

As we'll see in the next chapter, in phase two of Heaven, there'll be many different ministries and jobs to do in the Kingdom of God. There will be a great variety of functions, positions, and ministries for the saints to perform as we serve Christ in eternity. Notice here, that the one servant was placed over 10 cities, while the other was placed in a ruling capacity over 5 cities. They were both faithful, but to differing degrees, so they were each rewarded with different positions of responsibility in the Kingdom. This tells us that how we live and serve Jesus in the _present_, will determine how we're rewarded and promoted in the _future_ Kingdom. This is why it's of such crucial importance to consider this aspect of your Christian life _today_. Let me put it to you like this:

***Are you faithfully laboring for Jesus' Kingdom
with the resources He's entrusted to you?
Do you allow the thought of standing before
Jesus to receive crowns motivate you to
sacrificially serve Him now?***

This is the ultimate impact that the Judgement Seat of Christ should have upon the life of a believer. It should move us to live for Jesus zealously *today*, knowing that it will directly impact my *future* in the Kingdom. The promise of crowns should energize us to use our *present* position to make *future* provision in Heaven! (Read Luke 16:1-10)

What About Angels (And Demons) In Heaven?

For your own growth and personal study, I challenge you to read through the visions of two other men who were given a sneak peek into the Dimension of Heaven: the prophets Ezekiel and Isaiah. Be sure to read Ezekiel 1 and 10, along with Isaiah 6. Both contain many similarities to John's vision of the Throne Room, here in Revelation.

Also, to gain more insight into some of the angelic activity (including demons) that currently takes place before the Throne of God, be sure to read Job 1 and 2, along with 1 Kings 22:19-23. Even in our present time, satan still has access to the Throne of God, to ask permission to afflict and tempt certain believers! (Luke 22:31)

In this Dimension of Heaven, you'll see your loved ones who've passed on and knew Christ as Savior; you'll meet the Old Testament saints who died in faith; you'll fellowship with the Christians who've lived and died since the beginning of the Church 2,000 years ago; and you'll be in the midst of innumerable battalions of warrior angels – all worshipping the LORD and casting their crowns before Him in humble adoration! It will be a glorious reunion of believing families, and the ultimate worship concert of the ages, as we see the LORD face to Face – finally! Jesus described it with these beautiful words:

"Then I looked, and I heard the voice of many angels around the throne, the living creatures, and the elders; and the number of them was ten thousand times ten thousand, and thousands of thousands saying with a loud voice:

"Worthy is the Lamb who was slain to receive power and riches and wisdom, And strength and honor and glory and blessing!"
– Revelation 5:11-12 NKJV

This is the 1st Phase of the plan of Heaven that we'll experience. We will stay in the Dimension of Heaven worshipping, serving, fellowshipping, and enjoying God's tangible presence. This will continue until the 7 year Tribulation period is finished and completed on earth (Revelation 6-18), and this Christ-rejecting sinful world has been judged once and for all. When this is finished and over, the saints will then leave this unique Dimension of Heaven, and join Jesus in a climactic event known as the "Second Coming" of Christ. However, this takes us into the 2nd Phase of God's eternal plan, the Kingdom of Heaven coming to the earth!

Chapter 3

Phase #2: The Kingdom of Heaven

As we said, when the Tribulation Period is finished, it will usher in a new and important stage in the plan of Heaven. Once the 7 years of Tribulation (Revelation 6-18) are completed and the earth has been judged for its wickedness, all the saints will follow Christ, leave the Dimension of Heaven, and physically return to the earth with King Jesus. This will usher in the 2nd Phase God's Plan, which we call the "Kingdom of Heaven." It begins with the Second Coming of Christ, and it's incredible drama is described in detail in Revelation 19, where we read these words:

"Now I saw heaven opened, and behold, a white horse. And He who sat on him was called Faithful and True, and in righteousness He judges and makes war. His eyes were like a flame of fire, and on His head were many crowns. He had a name written that no one knew except

Himself. He was clothed with a robe dipped in blood, and His name is called The Word of God. And the armies in heaven, clothed in fine linen, white and clean, followed Him on white horses. Now out of His mouth goes a sharp sword, that with it He should strike the nations. And He Himself will rule them with a rod of iron. He Himself treads the winepress of the fierceness and wrath of Almighty God. And He has on His robe and on His thigh a name written: KING OF KINGS AND LORD OF LORDS."
– Revelation 19:11-16 NKJV

Just as the 1st Phase of Heaven was summarized by the word *"adoration"*, the 2nd Phase can be described by the word *"domination."* The reason for this, is that King Jesus will come back to rule, reign, and dominate the earth. As so many of the Old Testament prophets foretold, Christ will take over the world, conquer His enemies, and rule the planet from His glorious Throne in Jerusalem!

What Will Earth Be Like In The Kingdom?
This 2nd Phase of God's plan, the Kingdom of Heaven, is one of the most interesting time periods in all of the Bible. This phase answers the big question many of us have in our minds, when imagining Heaven:

"What will it be like, when the Kingdom of Heaven comes to earth?

The first element that will initiate this phase of Heaven, is the Return of Christ to the earth. The Kingdom of Heaven coming down, begins when the King Himself returns to the planet, in power and glory, to rule and reign. The King brings His Kingdom with Him, and once it arrives, it will be here forever! This is the moment where the Lord again resumes His rightful place of Lordship and Kingship over the world, and it will be a marvelous event to behold!

This long-awaited event is the fulfillment of hundreds of biblical prophecies, and is the main focus of the chapters on Heaven in the Bible. As a matter of fact, this period of the thousand-year reign of Christ on earth, is the most often described period of human history, in all of the Scriptures! It's obvious to see, that this event is of extreme importance to the heart of God, and it should be to us as well. It is one of the most anticipated moments in all of history – when GOD Himself comes down, in power and glory, to rule and reign over the earth!

As a Christian, when your imagination drifts off into daydreaming, I hope *this* is what you'll think about. When you have those hard days in life where you feel like just quitting and giving up, I encourage you to "fantasize" about *this* event – the Kingdom of Heaven coming to earth! I truly believe that if you comprehend the 2nd Phase of Heaven, it can serve as great fuel for your biblical *imagination*, and give you tremendous *inspiration* during dark days and hard times. It will help you to keep pressing forward, knowing the glorious things the Lord has in store for the future of our world!

<u>When Will The Kingdom Of Heaven Begin?</u>
This 2nd Phase of Heaven commences with the return of the King to the earth, as described in Revelation 19. The Second Coming of Christ initiates the Kingdom of God coming to the earth. Remember how John described it in his vision:

"Now I saw heaven opened, and behold, a white horse. And He who sat on him was called Faithful and True, and in righteousness He judges and makes war."
– Revelation 19:11 NKJV

As I understand this and picture it in my mind's eye, the sky will likely tear open and, pouring out of the Dimension of Heaven, the saints will come down, in battle formation, riding flying horses, for a heavenly "invasion" of planet earth, led at the front by King Jesus Himself! Christ will come to the battle of Armageddon, and wipe out His enemies with ease.

Interestingly, many Christians are opposed to the idea of war, claiming pacifism is the only biblical option for believers. While it's true that mankind has a gruesome tendency for cruelty in a time of war, the Bible fully endorses the professions of a soldier or police officer, and going to combat when ordered to. (Read Romans 13:1-7; Genesis 9:6; 1 Peter 2:13,14)

However, the Lord Jesus is no pacifist when it comes to destroying evil and conquering tyranny. Here, He is beautifully and boldly portrayed as our Great Commander and Conquering King in battle (Exodus 15:3)! Another ruler, king David of Israel, prophetically described this event almost a millennia before the birth of Jesus. David wrote this:

"Lift up your heads, O you gates! And be lifted up, you everlasting doors! And the King of glory shall come in. Who is this King of glory? The LORD strong and mighty, The LORD mighty in battle. Lift up your heads, O you gates! Lift up, you everlasting doors! And the King of glory shall come in. Who is this King of glory? The LORD of hosts, He is the King of glory."
– Psalm 24:7-10 NKJV

King David, who was familiar with war and the dangers of combat, describes Jesus in His Second Coming as our *"King of Glory"* who is *"..strong and mighty, the LORD mighty in battle."* What a great description of Jesus! He isn't portrayed as the gentle Lamb of God, sacrificed for the sins of the world. In contrast, here He is the Lion of Judah who destroys His enemies, and all who've opposed the rule of God upon the earth!

This is the first act of the 2nd Phase of Heaven. Jesus, in this war-like return to the earth, will destroy His enemies at the battle of Armageddon, He will ride into the city of Jerusalem, transforming it into the capital city of His glorious Kingdom, lasting for a 1,000 years!

How Long Will The Millennium Last?
During this 2nd Phase, the Kingdom of Heaven, Jesus will exalt His Church to rule and reign beside Him for a period of 1,000 years. Just as a king rules

with his queen at his side, so King Jesus will rule the world, with His Bride alongside Him.

Another chapter that describes this time period is Revelation 20. The age of the Millennium is explained in further detail, when John tells us this:

"Then I saw an angel coming down from heaven, having the key to the bottomless pit and a great chain in his hand. He laid hold of the dragon, that serpent of old, who is the Devil and Satan, and bound him for a thousand years; and he cast him into the bottomless pit, and shut him up, and set a seal on him, so that he should deceive the nations no more till the thousand years were finished. But after these things he must be released for a little while. And I saw thrones, and they sat on them, and judgment was committed to them. Then I saw the souls of those who had been beheaded for their witness to Jesus and for the word of God, who had not worshiped the beast or his image, and had not received his mark on their foreheads or on their hands. And they lived and reigned with Christ for a thousand years. But the rest of the dead did not live again until the thousand years were finished. This is the first resurrection."
– Revelation 20:1-5 NKJV

Will the Millennium Be 1,000 Literal Years?!?

We can learn numerous details about the Millennium from these verses. First of all, we can easily see how long the Millennium will last for – 1,000 years. Again, the word *"millennium"* itself means a thousand years, but in this chapter, it is stated very clearly. No less than six times does it say that this 2nd Phase of Heaven will last for a thousand years. There are some Christians who seem confused about this but if the Lord has told us *"My children, I want you to know that the Millennium will last for 1,000 years... 1,000 years... 1,000 years... 1,000 years... 1,000 years... 1,000 years!"* then that's exactly what He meant! It doesn't matter if some don't believe this (such as Martin Luther or John Calvin), it's what God's Word clearly teaches.

Will There Be World Peace In The Millennium?

Another interesting detail that we see, is that Satan will be "bound" during the Millennium. He will be captured and confined for the entire duration of this 1,000 years of the Kingdom of Heaven. This is what John described when he said:

"Then I saw an angel coming down from heaven, having the key to the bottomless pit and a great chain in his hand. He laid hold of the dragon, that serpent of old, who is the Devil and Satan, and bound him for a thousand years; and he cast him into the bottomless pit, and shut him up, and set a seal on him, so that he should deceive the nations no more till the thousand years were finished. But after these things he must be released for a little while."
– Revelation 20:1-3 NKJV

Today, satan and his minions are having a field day on planet earth. Contrary to the opinion of many religious people (and some confused Christians), satan is not ruling in Hell on a black obsidian throne. Though this is the "Looney Tunes" theology many people believe, it is definitely not the case! He is alive and well, and very active on the world scene today. In Job, the oldest book of the Bible, the Lord asked satan where he'd recently been operating:

"And the LORD said to Satan, 'From where do you come?' So Satan answered the LORD and said, 'From going to and fro on the earth, and from walking back and forth on it.'"
– Job 1:7 NKJV

According to the Bible, though Satan has lost his position and has become the Enemy of God's people, he still has access to Heaven to make requests for temptation. Satan is also fully operating on the world scene, transforming it into a cosmic battle ground, by causing war, disease, famine, persecution, and worldly perversions.

However, during the Millennium, this will all drastically change. Satan will be imprisoned and confined for the entire period of 1,000 years. Revelation 20 tells us that a mighty heavenly angel will take satan, and forcibly incarcerate him in the bottomless pit:

"And I saw an angel come down from heaven, having the key of the bottomless pit and a great chain in his hand. And he laid hold on the dragon, that old serpent, which is the Devil, and Satan, and bound him a thousand years, And

> ***cast him into the bottomless pit, and shut him
> up, and set a seal upon him, that he should
> deceive the nations no more, till the thousand
> years should be fulfilled: and after that
> he must be loosed a little season."
> - Revelation 20:1-3 NKJV***

This means that the Kingdom of Heaven will be a time of unparalleled peace and safety on planet earth. If the Destroyer is locked away, and incarcerated so that he can't escape to cause violence, bloodshed, war, etc... then it's obvious that the Millennium will be a glorious time of prosperity and physical peace, as we've never known since the Fall of Adam!

It's commonly stated that out of the 4,000 years of recorded human history, there have only been about 250 years of peace on planet earth. Incredible! War has almost been a constant feature of our human experience. At any given moment, there are dozens of wars and armed conflicts raging all over the globe!

But imagine what it will be like to finally have _world peace_ ... and for 1,000 years! Imagine how beautiful it will be to leave the keys in your car (if we still use cars) when you go to the store? How great will it feel to be able to leave your house unlocked at night, or not be afraid that you'll get mugged at the ATM machine? When the influence of satan is removed from the earth, the Millennium will be a glorious, peaceful time for the entire world. Nations won't wage war, terrorism will be a thing of the past, robberies and muggings will vanish, and murder and rape will not occur anymore! No wonder Jesus is called the *"Prince of Peace"* in Isaiah 9:6, for when He comes to rule and reign in the Kingdom of Heaven, there will be *global peace* like never before!

<u>Who Will Rule In The Millennium?</u>
A final observation that we can make about Revelation 20 is how it describes the saints and the followers of Christ. John wrote:

"And I saw thrones, and they sat on them, and judgment was committed to them. ...And they lived and reigned with Christ for a thousand years. But the rest of the dead did not live again until the thousand years were finished. This is the first resurrection."
– Revelation 20:4-5 NKJV

As we discussed earlier, Christians will rule the world at the side of Jesus in this period of the Millennium. The Church will be exalted, as the Bride of Christ, to rule at the side of Jesus. He will be the supreme God-King but we will be lesser kings and queens under Him, ruling and reigning at His side for a 1,000 years!

A reference is also made to the physical resurrection of believers, so let's briefly discuss it. It's an important aspect of understanding your life in the Millennial Kingdom. Paul described the physical resurrection of Christians when he taught us:

"But I do not want you to be ignorant, brethren, concerning those who have fallen asleep, lest you sorrow as others who have no hope. For if we believe that Jesus died and rose again, even

Phase #2: The Kingdom of Heaven

so God will bring with Him those who sleep in Jesus. For this we say to you by the word of the Lord, that we who are alive and remain until the coming of the Lord will by no means precede those who are asleep. For the Lord Himself will descend from heaven with a shout, with the voice of an archangel, and with the trumpet of God. And the dead in Christ will rise first. Then we who are alive and remain shall be caught up together with them in the clouds to meet the Lord in the air. And thus we shall always be with the Lord. Therefore, comfort one another with these words."
– 1 Thessalonians 4:13-18 NKJV

<u>What Will Our Bodies Be Like In Heaven?</u>

What Paul is teaching about is an event known as the *"Rapture"* of the Church. This comes from the Greek word *"harpazo"* for the English *"caught up"* in verse 17. The Latin word is *"raptus"* from which we get *"rapture"*. This word means to be "snatched away forcibly, caught away, pulled away, plucked up." In the Rapture, Jesus will secretly appear in the atmosphere, before the Tribulation begins, to take away the Church into the Dimension of Heaven. Paul also describes the Rapture in 1 Corinthian 15:51-58; Romans 5:9; 1 Thessalonians 1:10 and 5:9. Jesus spoke of it to his disciples in John 14:1-3 and Revelation 3:10 as well.

So, when you picture yourself in the Millennium, ruling and reigning alongside of your glorious King, envision yourself in a glorified, resurrected body of

75

power and strength. Paul described the future resurrection body of the saints like this:

> *"Behold, I tell you a mystery: We shall not all sleep, but we shall all be changed — in a moment, in the twinkling of an eye, at the last trumpet. For the trumpet will sound, and the dead will be raised incorruptible, and we shall be changed. For this corruptible must put on incorruption, and this mortal must put on immortality."*
> *– 1 Corinthians 15:51-53 NKJV*

Your glorified body, which you'll receive in the Rapture, will be just like the resurrected body of Jesus: free of decay, deterioration, sickness, or sin. It will be at optimal health and vitality, and probably of a median human age (in your prime). It will be a physical body that will be capable of eating and drinking food, although you won't necessarily need them, and it will be able to interact with the world around you in the Kingdom Age. (Read 1 John 3:1-3)

I believe you will be able to do such *amazing* things in this glorified body, that if you could see them now, they would appear supernatural or even superhuman! Actually, Paul uses those very words in describing the resurrection body in 1 Corinthians 15. He uses the words *"soma pneumatikon"* literally meaning *"a spiritual and supernatural/superhuman body."* It's interesting that the body of Jesus could apparently *move instantaneously* at the speed of thought (Luke 24:36-37), *disappear* at will (Luke 24:30-31), and even *fly* through the sky!

Since we're told that our bodies will be just like our Lord's, this is <u>*very*</u> exciting to say the least! John tells us this about our resurrection bodies in the Kingdom:

> **"Beloved, now we are children of God; and it has not yet been revealed what we shall be, but we know that when He is revealed, we shall be like Him, for we shall see Him as He is."**
> **– 1 John 3:2 NKJV**

Essentially, whatever you can see Jesus doing in His resurrection body, know that Scripture teaches you'll have one just like it, making the Kingdom of Heaven even more amazing. What a glorious future to look forward to! (Read Philippians 3:21)

What About Heaven In The Old Testament?

Many people wonder if it's only the New Testament that speaks of Heaven, or if the Old Testament does as well. Actually, the 39 books of the Old Testament Scriptures teach us more about Heaven, by far, that the New Testament! This is definitely the case concerning this 2nd Phase of God's Eternal Plan – the Kingdom of Heaven.

If we were to make a short list of where we can learn specific details about the Millennium, it would include notable Old Testament chapters such as:

- *Jeremiah 3; 23; 30-31*
- *Ezekiel 34; 40-48*
- *Daniel 2; 7; 12*
- *Hosea 1; 2; 14*
- *Zechariah 14*

- **Joel 3**
- **Amos 1; 9**
- **Nahum 1**
- **Habakkuk 3**
- **Haggai 2**
- **Micah 1; 4**

However, if we could choose only one book in the Old Testament to study the Kingdom of God, we would have to pick the book of Isaiah. Unlike any other book in the Bible, Isaiah contains an unparalleled amount of specific details about the Millennial reign of Jesus over the earth. Here is a sampling of the _huge_ amount of information in Isaiah, that can teach us about this 2nd Phase of Heaven:

Book of Isaiah – Millennial Chapters:
2, 4, 9, 11, 26, 32, 33, 35, 40, 42, 52, 56, 49, 60, 61, 62, 64, 65, 66

As you can see, the book of Isaiah is by far the single greatest storehouse of biblical information about the Millennium! Let's now examine a few other books from the Old Testament, to see what we can learn from them. But we'll finish off our study of the Millennium by diving into some of these great chapters from Isaiah – and you will be amazed what he reveals to us about Heaven!

The Millennium As Described By Daniel

The Kingdom of God coming to the earth, is an incredibly important concept throughout the Scriptures. As a matter of fact, it's considered by many theologians and Bible scholars to be the second most important theme in the entire Bible!

Of course, the first and foremost theme is GOD. The Bible is a book all about Him, His plan, His love, and His character. But right after this, the establishment of the Kingdom of Heaven upon the earth, is the most important theme in both the Old and New Testament.

Daniel is one of many Old Testament prophets who writes about this. If you are unfamiliar with this great book, I'd highly recommend getting familiar with it. Daniel's writings are perhaps the most important prophecies in the Old Testament, and without them, we wouldn't even understand the book of Revelation!

When it comes to the Millennium, Daniel has much to teach us as well. To start, let's examine the second chapter of his book, where he interprets the dream of Nebuchadnezzar, the king of Babylon. Daniel described the dream like this:

"You watched while a stone was cut out without hands, which struck the image on its feet of iron and clay, and broke them in pieces. Then the iron, the clay, the bronze, the silver, and the gold were crushed together, and became like chaff from the summer threshing floors; the wind carried them away so that no trace of them was found. And the stone that struck the image became a great mountain and filled the whole earth. ..."And in the days of these kings the God of heaven will set up a kingdom which shall never be destroyed; and the kingdom shall not be left

to other people; it shall break in pieces and consume all these kingdoms, and it shall stand forever. Inasmuch as you saw that the stone was cut out of the mountain without hands, and that it broke in pieces the iron, the bronze, the clay, the silver, and the gold—the great God has made known to the king what will come to pass after this. The dream is certain, and its interpretation is sure."
– Daniel 2:34-35, 44-45 NKJV

Nebuchadnezzar, the king of ancient Babylon from 605BC to 562BC, had a strange dream of a statue composed of different metals, that needed interpretation. Daniel the prophet, revealed to him that the LORD God had shown the king the 5 major world empires, that would arise over the globe in the future: Babylon, Medo-Persia; Greece; Rome; and a "Revived Rome." Amazingly, history has unfolded just as Daniel's prophecy predicted it would! This chapter is surely one of the greatest prophecies in the Bible, and it irrefutably proves the divine inspiration of the Scriptures!

Regarding the Millennium, Daniel tells the king that it will cover the earth in the days of the 5th world kingdom – a "revived" Roman Empire. Just as the metal statue in his dream had 10 toes, this last "revived" Roman Empire would have 10 kings ruling over it. Daniel declared in verse 44:

"...in the days of these kings the God of heaven will set up a kingdom which shall never be destroyed; and the kingdom shall not be left

to other people; it shall break in pieces and consume all these kingdoms, and it shall stand forever."
– Daniel 2:44 NKJV

This is describing the Kingdom of Heaven – the Millennium! It tells us some interesting information about the 1,000 year reign of Christ: it will arise when there is a global government divided in power between "10 kings"–a "revived" Roman Empire. According to many great Bible scholars and theologians, *today* we find ourselves on the verge of such a world government being established. As I look around at the United Nations, the International Monetary Fund, and the constant push towards "Globalism" in politics and economics, I have to agree. The Rapture, Second Coming, and Millennium are likely close at hand!

Another place we gain insight into the 2nd Phase of Heaven is in chapter 7 of Daniel's prophecy. It's very similar to the vision of chapter 2, but instead of seeing *metals*, Daniel sees *monsters*. After his vision of these monsters (representing world empires) he declares this regarding the Millennium:

"I was watching in the night visions, and behold, One like the Son of Man, coming with the clouds of heaven! He came to the Ancient of Days, and they brought Him near before Him. Then to Him was given dominion and glory and a kingdom, that all peoples, nations, and languages should serve Him. His dominion is an everlasting dominion, which shall not pass away, and His

kingdom the one which shall not be destroyed."
*** – Daniel 7:13,14 NKJV***

Daniel has a vision of the Messiah coming, defeating the last world empire, and establishing the Kingdom of Heaven on the earth! The One mentioned here as "the Son of Man" is none other than Jesus Christ. How do we know that? Because Jesus called himself the "Son of Man" more than 80 times in the Gospels. This was His favorite title for Himself, the "Son of Man." The Son of Man is here portrayed as a type of heavenly "Superman", who rips out of the Dimension of Heaven, defeats the Antichrist and his government, and rules over the entire earth!

Daniel had seen many kings and kingdoms rise and fall. He himself served in 3 different governments during his own lifetime. Daniel was in the Babylonian administration, then the Medes, and later the Persians. In his visions, Daniel even saw the rise and fall of Greece, and the Roman Empire. Many kings and kingdoms have risen and fallen throughout history, and this is all within God's sovereign power. But there is one special *King* and one unique *Kingdom* that is coming, and it will never come to an end! This is why Daniel said:

"...to Him was given dominion and glory and a kingdom, that all peoples, nations, and languages should serve Him. His dominion is an everlasting dominion, which shall not pass away, and His kingdom the one which shall not be destroyed."
*** – Daniel 7:14 NKJV***

This is what you should think of when you envision the Kingdom of Heaven. All peoples, all nations all, languages will serve Jesus Christ, our Great King! His Kingdom is the one which shall never be destroyed. That is what you should picture when you daydream about the Kingdom of Heaven...and I hope you do it often!

The Millennium As Described By Zechariah

Zechariah, another notable Old Testament prophet, also had very interesting visions, and wrote much about the Kingdom of Heaven. He described this 2nd Phase of God's plan in many places. In chapter 6 of his prophecy, he described the government of Christ like this:

"Thus says the LORD of hosts, saying: "Behold, the Man whose name is the BRANCH! From His place He shall branch out, And He shall build the temple of the LORD; Yes, He shall build the temple of the LORD. He shall bear the glory, and shall sit and rule on His throne; So He shall be a priest on His throne, and the counsel of peace shall be between them both."
– Zechariah 6:12,13 NKJV

We can see that during the Millennium Jesus will have many special names He'll go by. One of them is "the Branch". This is very fitting, as Christ is the One bearing the fruit of God's Kingdom on earth. It's interesting to remember that Jesus also called us "branches" and Himself "the Vine", from which we will bear fruit if we simply abide in Him on a daily basis. (Read John 15:1-5)

From this passage in Zechariah, we also learn that Jesus will build the Temple of the Lord in Jerusalem during the Kingdom Age, and He will rule the planet from His Throne there. This Temple, also mentioned by Ezekiel and John, is called the "Millennial Temple", and will be absolutely enormous in size! It will be over 12 times the size of Solomon's Temple, and well over 4 times larger than even Herod's Temple and all of it's courtyards! This Millennial Temple's court-yards are measured to be about 1 square mile in size, larger than the entire city of ancient Jerusalem. Simply amazing!

Zechariah declares that from this glorious Millennial Temple, Jesus will rule and reign over the earth, as our Great Priest-King! Christ is uniquely qualified for this, as He alone is proclaimed in the Scriptures to be our divine Prophet, King, and Priest. The writer of Hebrews declares that Jesus is currently serving His people as the Great High Priest, in the Heavenly Temple:

"And inasmuch as He was not made priest without an oath (for they have become priests without an oath, but He with an oath by Him who said to Him: "The LORD has sworn and will not relent, 'You are a priest forever According to the order of Melchizedek' "), by so much more Jesus has become a surety of a better covenant. Also there were many priests, because they were prevented by death from continuing. But He, because He continues forever, has an

unchangeable priesthood. Therefore, He is also able to save to the uttermost those who come to God through Him, since He always lives to make intercession for them. For such a High Priest was fitting for us, who is holy, harmless, undefiled, separate from sinners, and has become higher than the heavens..."
– Hebrews 7:20-26 NKJV

Presently, Jesus _serves_ us from the Dimension of Heaven as our Great High Priest; but prophetically, Jesus will _rule_ over us in the Kingdom of Heaven, as our Great Priest-King, according to Zechariah!

A final vision of the Kingdom in Zechariah's prophecy, is in chapter 14. He describes some interesting aspects of life in the city of Jerusalem, during the Millennium. He writes this:

"...the LORD my God will come, And all the saints with You. ... And the LORD shall be King over all the earth. In that day it shall be -"The LORD is one," And His name one. ... And it shall come to pass that everyone who is left of all the nations which came against Jerusalem shall go up from year to year to worship the King, the LORD of hosts, and to keep the Feast of Tabernacles. And it shall be that whichever of the families of the earth do not come up to Jerusalem to worship the King, the LORD of hosts, on them there will be no rain. If the family of Egypt will not come up and enter in, they shall have no rain; they shall receive the plague with which the LORD strikes the nations who do not come up to keep

*the Feast of Tabernacles. This shall be the
punishment of Egypt and the punishment of
all the nations that do not come up to keep the
Feast of Tabernacles."*
- Zechariah 14:5, 8-9, 16-19 NKJV

Here we see some fascinating aspects of the Millennium and what it will look like on a social level, for the people of Jerusalem and other cities in the Kingdom. First, Zechariah mentions that Christ will return the earth with His saints, and be the undisputed God-King over all the earth.

Next, he declares that the LORD is the only One that will be worshipped by humanity. The adoration of Yahweh, the LORD God of Israel – Father, Son, and Spirit – will be the global religion of mankind in the Millennium. Also, we learn that King Jesus will institute the yearly celebration of the Feast of Tabernacles (Leviticus 23) in Jerusalem. Every nation on the earth will send delegates to the city of Jerusalem to celebrate and keep this Feast...or they'll get no rain in their country!

As is always the case, it's worth it to worship the Lord continually – especially in the Millennium! However, if you don't want to be "spiritually dry" right now, worship Jesus every day of your life, and you'll be refreshed by the living waters of His Spirit and His Word in your heart!

The vision of the Kingdom of Heaven, as described by Zechariah is simply breathtaking: Jesus, as Priest-King ruling over the world from the Millennial Temple in Jerusalem, with the saints at His side; global worshippers streaming yearly to the

Temple to keep the Feast of Tabernacles; a world that is completely united in the exclusive worship of the One True God – the LORD. No wonder Jesus taught us to pray "...your Kingdom come...", as this will be the greatest time ever, to be alive on planet earth!

The Millennium As Described By Isaiah

Though every book of Scripture is valuable and priceless, some are unique in the amount of revelation and insight they give us. Isaiah is such a book. It is simply one of the most magnificent books in all of the Bible. Especially concerning the topic of the Millennium, as it contains dozens of chapters detailing this 2nd Phase of Heaven.

Isaiah is called a "Little Bible" by many teachers. This is due to the fact that Isaiah has sixty-six chapters–the same number of chapters as books in the Bible. Another similarity, is that after the 39th book of the Old Testament (Malachi), the grace of the New Testament begins with the Gospel of Matthew. Likewise, after the 39th chapter of Isaiah, comes grace in chapter 40. It is, in a very real sense, a "Little Bible" due to these fascinating similarities!

Many Bible teachers refer to Isaiah as the "Fifth Gospel." This is because Isaiah writes more about Jesus than any other biblical writer, except the Gospels of the New Testament. There are so many prophecies of Christ in this book, about 35 in total, it feels as though it belongs next to Matthew, Mark, Luke, and John!

Regarding the Millennium, no book in the entire Bible that can match Isaiah, in terms of sheer quantity on this theme. Let's look at some of the most powerful chapters from Isaiah's prophecy, and see what we can learn about the 2nd Phase of Heaven, from this great prophet.

Let me start with one of the early chapters of Isaiah, which paints a beautiful and colorful picture of the Kingdom of God on earth. Isaiah describes it like this:

"The word that Isaiah the son of Amoz saw concerning Judah and Jerusalem. Now it shall come to pass in the latter days that the mountain of the LORD's house shall be established on the top of the mountains, and shall be exalted above the hills; and all nations shall flow to it. Many people shall come and say, "Come, and let us go up to the mountain of the LORD, To the house of the God of Jacob; He will teach us His ways, and we shall walk in His paths." For out of Zion shall go forth the law, And the word of the LORD from Jerusalem. He shall judge between the nations, and rebuke many people; They shall beat their swords into plowshares, and their spears into pruning hooks; Nation shall not lift up sword against nation, neither shall they learn war anymore. O house of Jacob, come and let us walk in the light of the LORD."
– Isaiah 2:1-5 NKJV

We notice many details about the Millennium from what Isaiah writes. First of all, **the city of Jerusalem will be physically elevated and lifted up in altitude.** This is interesting, as we know from other scriptures (Zech 14:4) that there will be massive tectonic and geographical restructuring of our planet's surface, after the Tribulation and the return of Christ to the earth.

Also, we learn that **the Millennial Temple will be built on Mount Zion in Jerusalem.** This gigantic center of worship will be the main attraction in Jerusalem, the new capital city, in the most important country during the Kingdom Age. The importance of the Temple cannot be overstated, as it will function as the "Headquarters" of Jesus' earthly government during the Millennium!

<u>All For One, One For All!</u>

Furthermore, we can see that **all the nations of the earth will flow to Jerusalem** during this Kingdom Age, in order to worship the Lord and adore Him face to Face! Remember what the Paul told us in Philippians 2:9-11? He said that every knee will bow to Jesus and every tongue will confess He is the Lord. *This* will be the fulfillment of that famous statement! All nations will stream to Jerusalem and bow the knee to Christ! Can you imagine the Iraqis and Iranians, the Chinese and the Sudanese, all coming together to worship Jesus? There are many nations today that hate God, reject Christ, and persecute Christians mercilessly. But imagine this day when *all* nations of the earth, stream to Jerusalem to worship Christ as their Lord and King. What a glorious day it will be!

Will We Have Bible Study In Heaven?

Beyond this, we learn of something additional that worshippers will be engaging in: **the study of God's Word!** Just as we gather today, to study and learn God's Word, to know His mind and heart for our lives, we will continue to do so in the Kingdom of Heaven as well. The way Isaiah describes it show us that the people of the earth will have an earnest desire to hear from Christ, and learn His ways. They will eagerly travel to Jerusalem, with hungry hearts and minds, for the words of Jesus!

Wanted In Heaven: Bible Teachers?!?

It goes on to tell us that **the Word of the Lord will go out from Zion.** This may indicate that one of the special ministries in the Millennial Kingdom will be that of Bible teaching! Just as the Lord has seen fit to do in the Old and New Testaments, in the Kingdom of Heaven He will send teachers of His Word throughout His lands, to instruct the peoples in His perfect love towards them, and His eternal desires for them!

This means that good Bible teachers will have "job security" on into the Kingdom Age, as we continue to learn about the LORD forever and ever. Since God is infinite in His Being, there's an infinite amount for us to learn...and we'll never get to the end of it! Getting to know our God better and better will be the true adventure, in the Kingdom of Heaven!

Will There Be Disobedience In The Kingdom?

Isaiah goes on to tell us that the Lord "will judge between the nations." This means that beyond being our Great Priest-King, Jesus will also operate as the Great Judge over the peoples of the earth. He will mediate disagreements between nations and settle international disputes, as they occasionally arise throughout the Millennium. Christ will be the King of the Earth, but also the Judge of the earth during these 1,000 years. In the minds of many people, this raises the question:

"Will people disobey Christ during the Millennium?"

The answer is *"No"* and *"Yes"*, depending on which people you're talking about. The two broad groups of humans that will be present in the Millennial Kingdom are: 1) *Those with Resurrection bodies* 2) *Those without Resurrection bodies*. As we'll discover, whether or not a person has a resurrected body is the deciding factor of whether they *can* sin against the Lord, or *can't*. Those whose bodies are resurrected and glorified won't be engaging in sinful disobedience, because the very capability to sin will be absent in these new "upgraded" models (1John 3:2; Philippians 3:20,21).

Two Categories Of People In The Kingdom?!?

Now, the first group of humans, those *with* resurrected and glorified bodies, will be a combination of resurrected *Christians*, resurrected *Old Testament saints*, and resurrected *Tribulation saints*. These 3 groups will be obeying and serving the Lord continually, in their new Kingdom ministries, in perfected, glorified, and sinless bodies!

However, those people *without* glorified bodies, will be the problematic group during the Millennium. It appears that it will still be possible for this group of "normal" bodied humans to disobey Christ's commands during the Millennium. This group will still have the capacity to sin and disobey the Lord, if they choose to. They will be swiftly punished by the iron-clad "Justice System" of the Kingdom. This group of "normal" bodied people will be those who survive the Tribulation Period, and are allowed to enter the Millennial Kingdom, after successfully passing the "Judgement of Nations."

Jesus taught about this "Entrance Exam" into the Kingdom Age in Matthew 25:31-46. He described it like this:

"When the Son of Man comes in His glory, and all the holy angels with Him, then He will sit on the throne of His glory. All the nations will be gathered before Him, and He will separate them one from another, as a shepherd divides his sheep from the goats. And He will set the sheep on His right hand, but the goats on the left."
– Matthew 25:31-33 NKJV

This "Judgement of Nations" is where Christ will decide which of the unbelieving survivors of the Tribulation, will be allowed to enter His Millennial Kingdom, to enjoy the blessings and grace of God. Interestingly, if we read the rest of Matthew 25, we discover that the basis of their permission to enter is one simple criteria: ***How they treated Israel and the Jewish people during their lifetime!*** Based upon this, they will or won't be allowed into the glory of the Millennial Kingdom. (Read Genesis 12:3)

These "regular" humans who are not yet saved, will obviously have the ability and opportunity to accept Christ and be born again during the Millennial Kingdom (1 Timothy 2:3-5). Many of them will choose to do so, and become born again believers during these marvelous 1,000 years.

However, in terms of their outward behavior, it will be very similar to now. All people on planet earth will be forced to follow the "Law" of the Kingdom, and required to "bow the knee" to King Jesus, and His servants who rule over them. It will not be a Democracy in the Millennium, but rather a *Theocracy* – a holy Government and righteous Kingdom ruled by God Himself. The world will still be required to show active submission to the King of Love, whether they want to or not (Phil 2:9-11).

Though people's obedience will be required during the Millennium, in their hearts, many will still make the decision to reject Christ... and remain unsaved! Even though they've survived the Tribulation period, been allowed entrance into the Kingdom, will see a nearly perfect earth, watch glorified saints ruling and reigning all around them, and observe the angels of God soaring through the skies... they will *still* choose to reject Jesus and remain unsaved in their hearts!

This clearly reveals just how sinful, stubborn, and wicked the heart of man truly is. This group of unbelieving humans will become problematic over the course of the Millennium, and even stage a dramatic rebellion at the end of this period (Rev 20:7-9), which we will examine later. It is *this* category of people who will be judged by Jesus when necessary, and even punished for their crimes by His appointed servants in the Millennial Kingdom. (Read Revelation 2:26-29)

Marriages And Children In The Kingdom?!?

Another thing we learn about the "normal" humans in the Millennium is this: *They're still going to be able to have babies!* Since they won't possess resurrection bodies, the unbelieving humans of the Millennium will still be able to get married, sexually reproduce, and have children (Genesis 1:27,28; Hebrews 13:4). This won't be the case for the glorified saints, as we'll be "married" to Christ and serving Him continually! (Read Matthew 22:30; Mark 12:25; Ephesians 5:30-32).

However, these "normal" bodied humans will have a "Baby Boom" unlike any other time in history! Just imagine how many kids could be born during the Millennium – a world that is near perfect, completely at peace, with a total absence of war and violence, with plenty of food for all people, in a restored natural environment! During this period of the Millennial Kingdom, there will be a population explosion on planet earth like never before, and the world will be full of joyful, happy children, who are so precious to the Lord (Luke 18:16).

One Of The Greatest Ministries In The Kingdom!

Since there will be so many children born and raised in the Millennium, children's ministry will be one of the greatest ministries in the Kingdom of Christ. Just like today, all of these children will still need to be "evangelized" and taught the truth about

Jesus Christ and His saving work on the Cross for them. Other than Jesus, no human child is ever born saved, not even during the Millennium. This means that each and every one of them will need to be led to a saving knowledge of Christ and discipled to follow Him. Evangelism, and especially Children Evangelism, will be two of the most needed and vibrant ministries in the Millennial Kingdom. The Great Commission will still be in effect for Christians (Matthew 28:18-20; Mark 16:15), and we'll still be sharing the Gospel – even in this 2nd Phase of Heaven!

Will There Be War In The Millennium?

Going back to the Isaiah 2 passage, a final truth that we see about the Kingdom of Heaven, is that there will be international peace between the nations of the earth. Isaiah stated it like this:

"They shall beat their swords into plowshares, and their spears into pruning hooks; Nation shall not lift up sword against nation, neither shall they learn war anymore."
– Isaiah 2:4 NKJV

During the Millennial Kingdom, there will no longer be war between the countries of our planet. Nation will no longer fight against nation, nor train for war anymore. All of the money, energy, and resources that are used today for warfare, combat, and national defense will be funneled towards feeding the world, helping other people, and carrying out the Kingdom plans of our Great Ruler, Jesus Christ.

Do you know what building has this Bible verse engraved in it? The United Nations headquarters in Brussels, Belgium. The United Nations was established on October 24th, 1945 just after World War II. It was created in the hopes of preventing another catastrophic world conflict, where over 60 million people were killed. It was founded with 51 member states and, at the time of this writing, has 193. However, it is grossly ineffective and often impotent at maintaining peace in our world today. If it's left up to us, peace will never come to the earth!

Peace will finally arrive when the "Prince of Peace" comes, to rule and reign in the Kingdom of Heaven! When He does, Isaiah tells us that the nations will finally be at harmony with each other, and humans will train for war no longer. Global Peace will elude us forever until Jesus, the Great Prince of Peace, brings it to the earth in the Millennium!

What About Nature and Animals In The Millennium?

For those of us who love God's creation and the variety of animals on our planet, we often wonder how the Kingdom of Heaven will affect this part of our world. Isaiah speaks to this issue as well. In chapter 11 of his prophecy, Isaiah said this:

"But with righteousness He shall judge the poor, and decide with equity for the meek of the earth; He shall strike the earth with the rod of His mouth, and with the breath of His lips He shall slay the wicked. Righteousness shall be the belt of His loins, And faithfulness the belt of His waist. "The wolf also shall dwell with the lamb, the

leopard shall lie down with the young goat, the calf and the young lion and the fatling together; And a little child shall lead them. The cow and the bear shall graze; Their young ones shall lie down together; and the lion shall eat straw like the ox. The nursing child shall play by the cobra's hole, and the weaned child shall put his hand in the viper's den. They shall not hurt nor destroy in all My holy mountain, for the earth shall be full of the knowledge of the LORD as the waters cover the sea."
– Isaiah 11:4-9 NKJV

Isaiah describes the glorious rule and reign of Jesus in the Millennium. He will be the Judge who rules in fairness, equity, and justice. But Isaiah also gives us a wonderful insight into how the supernatural reign of Christ will affect all of nature, including the entire Animal Kingdom.

Amazingly, he declares that the animosity that now exists between creatures such as wolves and lambs, leopards and goats, cows and bears, even cobras and humans, will be *completely removed* during the Millennial Kingdom! He tells us that these creatures, and the rest of the animal kingdom, will have the animosity within them simply taken away. What an incredible time this will be on our world – animals of every kind will be gentle, safe, and completely approachable by humans!

The aggression we see in the animal world today was not created or designed by God. Scripture tells us that it came from the Fall of Adam, when sin entered the natural world. Genesis 3 tells us this:

"So the LORD God said to the serpent: "Because you have done this, you are cursed more than all cattle, and more than every beast of the field; On your belly you shall go, and you shall eat dust All the days of your life. And I will put enmity Between you and the woman, and between your seed and her Seed; He shall bruise your head, and you shall bruise His heel." To the woman He said: "I will greatly multiply your sorrow and your conception; In pain you shall bring forth children; Your desire shall be for your husband, and he shall rule over you." Then to Adam He said, "Because you have heeded the voice of your wife, and have eaten from the tree of which I commanded you, saying, 'You shall not eat of it': "Cursed is the ground for your sake; In toil you shall eat of it all the days of your life."
– Genesis 3:14-17 NKJV

In this book of Beginnings, we see that the sin of Adam infected and affected our world in many different ways. It changed the amount of pain that women experience during childbirth; the way that a wife looks at and longs for her husband; it increased the difficulty of producing crops from the ground, as it was cursed; but it also placed "enmity" or animosity between Eve and the serpent.

This aggression and animosity, resulting from Adam's sin (Romans 5), spread to all of God's creation, and infected the entire animal kingdom. This was the beginning of the bloodshed that we see in nature today. This is also when carnivorous (meat-eating) behavior began in the animal kingdom. Prior to this, all the animals that God created (even dinosaurs like T-Rex and Raptors) were herbivores, or plant eaters. Prior to this, all animals were at peace with each other and mankind, as there was no sin in the world. Everything was perfect in God's creation. But Adam's rebellion dramatically changed all that, and we've been living with the repercussions of his foolish decision for thousands of years!

However, Isaiah tells us that in the Millennium, the animals will return to their original state of herbivores, and being friendly to each other. He describes this fundamental change in animal behavior, when he writes:

"The wolf also shall dwell with the lamb, the leopard shall lie down with the young goat, the calf and the young lion and the fatling together; And a little child shall lead them. The cow and the bear shall graze; Their young ones shall lie down together; and the lion shall eat straw like the ox. The nursing child shall play by the cobra's hole, and the weaned child shall put his hand in the viper's den."
– Isaiah 11:6-8 NKJV

Wolves and lambs will be playmates; leopards and goats will sleep next to each other; baby calfs and lions will lay side by side; cows and bears will feed together in the fields; lions will eat straw just like an ox does; and best of all, little children will be able to safely have fun with all of them, even playing with snakes like the cobra! What an amazing time this will be on planet earth!

Today there are places in Tibet and the far east where you can go and play with wild tigers out in the open – but it's not 100% safe. I think I'd rather wait and take my chances with the lions, tigers, and bears of the Millennium! They'll all be transformed into playful, kind, and gentle creatures once again, for all humans to enjoy! (Read Isaiah 65:25)

As many children dream of when they hear the "Chronicles of Narnia", in this beautiful day, all of God's amazing creatures will be our playmates and gentle companions, as we enjoy the wonders of the Kingdom of Heaven… on the earth!

Will There Be "Blessed" Countries In The Millennium?

As we've already seen, there will be a multiplicity of nations in the Kingdom of Heaven, when it covers the earth. Jesus will be the Great King over the planet (Zechariah 14:9) and the saints will function as lesser kings and queens, ruling and reigning at His side (Revelation 2:26-28).

However, it's intriguing to realize that there are specific countries Isaiah mentions by name that will enjoy a position of "blessedness" and prominence in the Millennial Kingdom. Most of us already understand that Israel will be the greatest and most exalted nation on the earth, for Jesus will rule and reign from there, in His Kingdom capital – the city of Jerusalem. But Isaiah also tells us that there are other nations that will be blessed in a very special way. What he says may shock and surprise you! He tells us in chapter 19 of his prophecy:

"In that day five cities in the land of Egypt will speak the language of Canaan and swear by the LORD of hosts; one will be called the City of Destruction. In that day there will be an altar to the LORD in the midst of the land of Egypt, and a pillar to the LORD at its border. And it will be for a sign and for a witness to the LORD of hosts in the land of Egypt; for they will cry to the LORD because of the oppressors, and He will send them a Savior and a Mighty One, and He will deliver them. Then the LORD will be known to Egypt, and the Egyptians will know the LORD in that day, and will make sacrifice and offering; yes, they will make a vow to the LORD and perform it. And the LORD will strike Egypt, He will strike and heal it; they will return to the LORD, and He will be entreated by them and heal them. In that day there will be a highway from Egypt to Assyria, and the Assyrian will come into Egypt and the Egyptian into Assyria, and the Egyptians will serve with the Assyrians. In that day Israel will be one of three with Egypt and Assyria—a blessing in the midst of the land, whom the LORD of hosts shall bless, saying, 'Blessed is Egypt My people, and Assyria the work of My hands, and Israel My inheritance.'"
– Isaiah 19:18-25 NKJV

Unbeknownst to most Christians, during the Millennium, Egypt and Assyria (modern day Iran, Iraq, Turkey, and Syria) will enjoy a place of special blessing and favor in the Kingdom of Christ. Though each of these nations were hostile and antagonistic to the people of God in the Old Testament, when His Kingdom comes, Jesus will pour His grace upon all of them (as He has upon us) and transform the very fabric of their society! From this reference we learn numerous aspects of how the LORD will prosper these nations during the Millennium.

First, it appears that numerous cities will speak a special language of Canaan (possibly Hebrew), and swear loyalty to the LORD. Isaiah also tells us that there will be monuments of worship built to the LORD, specifically a pillar and altar of sacrifice.

Next, there will apparently be a conflict of some sort in this country, during which the people of Egypt will cry out to the LORD, who will send a *"deliverer"* to save them. This word in Hebrew is *"yasha"* and literally means a *"rescuer, deliverer, avenger, savior, or hero".* I personally believe that this is one of the saints who exercises a ministry of enforcing the LORD's justice and rule upon the earth, during the Kingdom Age (Rev 2:26-27; Obadiah 1:21). After this conflict is resolved, the entire nation of Egypt will turn to the LORD, and He will supernaturally heal their land from its negative condition.

Lastly, Isaiah says that some sort of "Super-Highway" will be built between Egypt and Assyria, a distance of over 1,100 kilometers or about 700 miles! These two nations will apparently go back and forth across this "Super-Highway", to serve the LORD and help each other's countries. This construction might be connected to Israel in some way, since Isaiah mentions a "Highway of Holiness" to be built there as well. In chapter 35 Isaiah says:

> *"A highway shall be there, and a road, and it shall be called the Highway of Holiness. The unclean shall not pass over it, but it shall be for others. Whoever walks the road, although a fool, shall not go astray. No lion shall be there, nor shall any ravenous beast go up on it; It shall not be found there. But the redeemed shall walk there, and the ransomed of the LORD shall return, and come to Zion with singing, with everlasting joy on their heads. They shall obtain joy and gladness, and sorrow and sighing shall flee away."*
> *– Isaiah 35:8-10 NKJV*

Isaiah concludes this fascinating passage on Egypt by telling us that ultimately, Egypt, Assyria, and Israel will all enjoy a special position of blessing and grace:

> *"In that day Israel will be one of three with Egypt and Assyria—a blessing in the midst of the land, whom the LORD of hosts shall bless, saying, 'Blessed is Egypt My people, and Assyria the work of My hands, and Israel My inheritance.'"*
> *– Isaiah 19:24-25 NKJV*

The Grace of God is so obvious in every book of the Bible, but especially in a passage like this! What amazing kindness the LORD will pour out on these nations, to the point that He transforms them into *"...My people...the work of My hands...My inheritance."* It reminds me of what Christ has done for each of us, by washing us in His blood, and transforming us by His Spirit. Even in the Millennium, if any man is in Christ, he can become a new creation with a new beginning! (2 Corinthians 5:17)

Will There Be Handicapped People In The Kingdom?
One of the greatest pains that we have in today's fallen world, is in seeing our loved one's and others around us, struggle with illnesses, diseases, handicaps, and infirmities. It's estimated by some that there are 150 million people in the world today that suffer from some sort of significant disability in their lives. Over 30 million people worldwide suffer from cancer. All of this causes tremendous pain and heartache in our minds, as well as in the heart of God.

But in the Kingdom of Heaven, this will forever change! Like the sun shining on a heavy fog in a dark valley, causing it to dissipate and vanish, so the Son of God will shine His grace upon this world in the Millennium, and thereby eradicate sickness, handicaps, and disease from our planet! In chapter 35 of his prophecy, Isaiah goes on to say this:

"Say to those who are fearful-hearted, "Be strong, do not fear! Behold, your God will come with vengeance, with the recompense of God; He will come and save you." Then the eyes of the blind shall be opened, And the ears of the deaf shall be unstopped. Then the lame shall leap like a deer, And the tongue of the dumb sing. For waters shall burst forth in the wilderness, And streams in the desert. The parched ground shall become a pool, And the thirsty land springs of water; In the habitation of jackals, where each lay, there

shall be grass with reeds and rushes."
– Isaiah 35:4-7 NKJV

This is a chapter on the Millennial Kingdom that should be shared with anyone suffering from a debilitating physical condition in their life. Here we see the dramatic changes that Christ will perform as our "Great Physician" and the "LORD our Healer."

Blindness will be thing of the past, because the Light of world will give them new sight! Deafness will vanish away, for the One who fashioned the ear will graciously heal it. Lameness will be no more, as Jesus lifts people up by the power of His Spirit to run after Him and leap for joy in His presence! Those suffering from speech problems will be forever healed by the Word incarnate, Jesus Christ, and they'll sing and shout His praises in passionate worship!

The healing ministry of Jesus in His first coming was a small preview of what Isaiah saw here: the beautiful transformation of GOD's healing power, washing over a world plagued by sin, and making all things new with the health, vitality, and life of His Spirit! What Jesus did for selected people during His first coming, will be unleashed upon the entire planet in His Second Coming, to inaugurate the Kingdom of Heaven on earth!

How Long Will People Live In The Millennium?

One of the greatest questions that people ask concerning the Millennial Kingdom, is how long people will live for. This is a great question to consider, and the answer might surprise you. Of course, the resurrected saints will live forever in immortality, in their glorified bodies. We know this, because Paul the apostle declares it in 1 Corinthians 15 when he states:

"...in a moment, in the twinkling of an eye, at the last trumpet. For the trumpet will sound, and the dead will be raised incorruptible, and we shall be changed. For this corruptible must put on incorruption, and this mortal must put on immortality. So when this corruptible has put on incorruption, and this mortal has put on immortality, then shall be brought to pass the saying that is written: "Death is swallowed up in victory." – 1 Corinthians 15:52-54 NKJV

Based upon this and other verses in the New Testament, the questions of age and death do not apply to the resurrected saints. We'll be enjoying the vigor and vitality of our new glorified bodies. We'll be able to live and serve our great King, in power and strength, throughout the Kingdom of Heaven and on into the Eternal Heavens...forever!

However, those in the Kingdom of Heaven that still possess regular human bodies, will be affected to some degree, as their bodies will still be in the aging process and capable of dying. Let's examine a wonderful passage on the Millennium, the great chapter of Isaiah 65. He writes these words:

"But be glad and rejoice forever in what I create; For behold, I create Jerusalem as a rejoicing, And her people a joy. I will rejoice in Jerusalem,

*and joy in My people; The voice of weeping shall no longer be heard in her, Nor the voice of crying. "No more shall an infant from there live but a few days, nor an old man who has not fulfilled his days; For the child shall die one hundred years old, But the sinner being one hundred years old shall be accursed. They shall build houses and inhabit them; They shall plant vineyards and eat their fruit. They shall not build and another inhabit; They shall not plant and another eat; For as the days of a tree, so shall be the days of My people, And My elect shall long enjoy the work of their hands."
– Isaiah 65:18-22 NKJV*

There are good clues in this passage that we can learn from, regarding the possible age limit of "unglorified" humans during the Millennial Kingdom. First we see that, this is indeed speaking of the Millennium, because of how the Lord describes Jerusalem. He mentions "creating" Jerusalem as a "joy" and rejoicing" to His people, one that should cause gladness forever. This is clearly pointing to the future transformation of the beloved capital city in the Kingdom of Heaven.

Specifically, we are told that the common voice of "weeping" and "crying" over people's death, will not continually be heard as was the case in Isaiah's day. Rather that long lifespans will return to humanity during the Millennium, as they once did in the days before Noah's Flood. We're told in Genesis 5 that humans of that "Pre-Deluvian" age lived for centuries on the earth, with Methuselah growing to be the oldest man in the Scriptures, at 969 years old! Though this may seem incredible to some, it's taught here in a very literal sense, has always been accepted by the historical Christian church, and Isaiah seems to give it credence in this passage. Read his words again, regarding people's ages during the Millennium:

"No more shall an infant from there live but a few days, nor an old man who has not fulfilled his days; For the child shall die one hundred years old, But the sinner being one hundred years old shall be accursed."
– Isaiah 65:20 NKJV

At the very least, it teaches us that human lifespans will be much longer than they are now. This makes sense, as the earth itself will be greatly changed and improved during the Millennium, perhaps back to the environmental conditions of the early world of Genesis, before the Global Flood.

Some believe these references might mean that if the "unglorified" humans in the Millennium don't make a decision to come to Christ in salvation by the time they reach 100 years of age, they'll die suddenly! Though they lived their lives in outward obedience to the King's laws (because it was mandatory), their sudden death will make it apparent that they were never saved, and not truly loyal to the King in their hearts. Though we can't say for sure, I think this is an interesting possibility to consider.

Regardless, we know that even for the "unglorified" humans, the Millennium will be a time of unparalleled blessing, joy, and long life. The wise among them will surely choose to accept Christ, be born again, and (eventually receiving glorified bodies) and live in the presence of their great God and Savior, Jesus Christ... forever!

Will Mankind Rebel During The Millennium?

As beautiful and wonderful as the Kingdom of Heaven will be, there will nonetheless be elements of it that are flawed. This is due to one simple reason: unsaved humans will be there!

Anytime unredeemed humans are a part of the picture, there will inevitably be problems and pain. As long as sinners are in the equation, there will always be a certain amount of disaster and death, for the end result of sin is always death (Romans 6:23). The Millennium will be no exception to this rule.

As incredible as it sounds, at the end of the Kingdom of Heaven, there will be a huge group of **"unglorified"** humans that stage a large-scale rebellion against Jesus Christ! Though these people have been born into this amazing Kingdom, have grown up seeing angels soar thru the skies, glorified saints ruling the world, and have known that Jesus reigns from the Temple in Jerusalem, they will ultimately choose to reject Christ! This will happen when satan is released at the end of the Millennium. He will go throughout the world and successfully deceive this huge group of "unglorified" humans, and lead them in an armed rebellion against the King in Jerusalem. Revelation chapter 20 describes it like this:

"Now when the thousand years have expired, Satan will be released from his prison and will go out to deceive the nations which are in the four corners of the earth, Gog and Magog, to gather them together to battle, whose number is as the sand of the sea. They went up on the breadth of the earth and surrounded the camp of the saints and the beloved city. And fire came down from God out of heaven and devoured them. The devil, who deceived them, was cast into the lake of fire and brimstone where the beast and the false prophet are. And they will be tormented day and night forever and ever. Then I saw a great white throne and Him who sat on it, from whose face the earth and the heaven fled away. And there was found no place for them. And I saw the dead, small and great, standing before God, and books were opened. And another book was opened, which is the Book of Life. And the dead were judged according to their works, by the things which were written in the books. The sea gave up the dead who were in it, and Death and Hades delivered up the dead who were in them. And they were judged, each one according to his works. Then Death and Hades were cast into the lake of fire. This is the second death. And anyone not found written in the Book of Life was cast into the lake of fire."
– Revelation 20:7-15 NKJV

This chapter describes the final and dramatic events of the Millennial Kingdom. Numerous things will be happening during this time, but we can summarize this climactic episode with two key concepts: **1)** *Confrontation* against the Lord **2)** *Condemnation* from the Lord. Let's examine each of them in turn, as we bring our study of the Millennium to a close.

#1–Confrontation against the Lord

The beginning of this fateful confrontation is the moment when satan is released from the bottomless pit. John, the writer of Revelation, tells us that the devil will deceive the nations and gather them to battle against the Lord Jesus. This should not surprise us as it has been one of satan's primary methods of attack from the very beginning, starting with Adam and Eve in the Garden (Genesis 3:1-7), and it continues to be so, up to our present day (John 8:44-45).

Some people ask the question *"But why in the world would God release satan from the bottomless pit? Why not just keep him locked up for all of eternity?"* Though the answer isn't explicitly given to us, we can venture some good guesses as to why the Lord will allow this.

Satan's release will demonstrate the WICKEDNESS of the devil.

Even after being incarcerated and confined for 1,000 years, this fallen angel will still be seething with hatred for his Creator, and venomous contempt for His prized creation: humans. There will have been no reform or correction in his behavior; no repentance or contrition for his evil actions down through the millennia. This appears to not even be possible for angels. Satan will still remain utterly opposed to God and will seek a last ditch effort to overthrow the righteous government of King Jesus – and will fail miserably in doing so! But forever, it will be echoed in the corridors of Heaven that satan was beyond hope, and was never going to change. His wickedness and evil will be apparent to everyone who remembers it – and so will be God's righteous anger in punishing him for eternity!

Satan's release will demonstrate the DEPRAVITY of man.

Another element that will be made obvious in this stage of the Millennium, will be the sinfulness and depravity of unsaved mankind. You wouldn't think it possible for humans to turn away from God Himself in the flesh, ruling and reigning visibly on the earth... but it will be. The sinfulness of man runs so deep that even in this near-perfect environment of the Kingdom, complete with the glorified saints, billions of angels, and the glory of God, they will still have a desire for self-worship and personal idolatry! This shows us that it's not man's environment or external influences that determine his condition. When given the chance, millions of unglorified humans, living in the last decades of the Millennium, will rally to the call of satan (through a human leader titled "Gog") and militarily oppose Jesus Christ! Though we don't know what technology or weapons they'll try to assemble, it really doesn't matter in the end. They will be quickly and decisively vanquished by the King Himself, and finally evil will be put to an end... forever!

Satan's release will demonstrate the JUSTICE of God.

An important truth that will become apparent in this final confrontation of these human rebels, led by the Dragon, is the perfect Justice and righteous Judgement of God. As Jesus rains down fire upon them, vanquishing these foolish traitors, and eventually exiles them to the Lake of Fire, there will be no possibility to contest His decision. It will be obvious to all who've witnessed it, that the Lord Himself was "slow to anger" and extremely patient towards these people during the years of the Millennium, though they chose to reject His kindness repeatedly. When their rebellious hearts are finally revealed, and they choose to ally themselves with the Dragon, our King will be justified to punish them in righteous anger. God's Justice will be manifested in a glorious way, and for all of eternity, no creature will be able to question His righteous character. Rather, we will sing His praises and declare "...Just and True are your ways, O King of the saints!" (Read Revelation 15:3)

#2–Condemnation from the Lord

Another truth that emerges from this passage in Revelation 20 is the Final Judgement of the wicked, and their eternal punishment in the Lake of Fire. The ending of the Millennium will be the ultimate resolution to the "Problem of Evil" that has plagued mankind from the beginning. It is the well-deserved recompense of the wicked for their evil deeds, down through the centuries.

In the minds of many people today, as they look around the world, witnessing all the murders, rapes,

113

kidnappings, child abuse, wars, genocide, serial kill-ings, terrorism, and a thousand other crimes, the question arises in their minds:

"Why hasn't God punished evil people yet?"

This day, at the end of the Millennial Kingdom, will finally answer that age-old question. The wicked deeds of our present world that appear to have gone unpunished, will receive their full recompense and fierce retribution on this Day of Judgement. It's described in graphic detail by John:

"The devil, who deceived them, was cast into the lake of fire and brimstone where the beast and the false prophet are. And they will be tormented day and night forever and ever. Then I saw a great white throne and Him who sat on it, from whose face the earth and the heaven fled away. And there was found no place for them. And I saw the dead, small and great, standing before God, and books were opened. And another book was opened, which is the Book of Life. And the dead were judged according to their works, by the things which were written in the books. The sea gave up the dead who were in it, and Death and Hades delivered up the dead who were in them. And they were judged, each one according to his works. Then Death and Hades were cast into the lake of fire. This is the second death. And anyone not found written in the Book of Life was cast into the lake of fire."
– Revelation 20:10-15 NKJV

Punishment In Hell Doesn't Last Forever?!?

It's a great surprise to many Christians that Hell is not the final place of punishment for the wicked. Though many believers and even pastors commonly say **"You don't want to reject Jesus, or you'll spend an eternity in Hell!"**, it's not technically true according to the Scriptures. Though eternal punishment of the wicked is taught in the Bible, Hell is not the final destination of the unsaved – the Lake of Fire is! As we'll come to discover, it is a much worse fate than anything that could be imagined!

The next question is usually **"Where is the Lake of Fire located at?"** However, that is never specifically answered in the Bible. Some teachers will tell you that it's located in the center of the earth, others will say that it's inside a burning star, while others believe it to be a different dimension altogether. But truthfully, the specific answer is never declared in the Scriptures. The important truth about the Lake of Fire is not the _where_ but rather the _what_. Understanding what kind of a place it is, is the core issue regarding this eternal destination of the unsaved!

As described here, it is a Lake of **"fire"** and **"brimstone"** that is burning continually. The people that are cast into it will be punished **"day and night forever and ever."** These words are enough to make even the hardest heart weep over the fate of their unsaved friends and loved ones. Truly understanding and believing this doctrine of "Eternal Punishment of the Wicked", should motivate every believer to recommit themselves to reaching out, sharing with, and praying for their unsaved friends and family!

(How are you doing with that? Read Mark 16:15 and Acts 1:8)

Some Bible teachers try to interpret these verses "symbolically" or "allegorically", not believing this could ever be a literal event in the future. However, the Scriptures clearly teach the eternal punishment of the unrighteous. Christ Himself told us these words concerning the physical punishment of the wicked:

"If your hand causes you to sin, cut it off. It is better for you to enter into life maimed, rather than having two hands, to go to hell, into the fire that shall never be quenched–where 'Their worm does not die, And the fire is not quenched.' And if your foot causes you to sin, cut it off. It is better for you to enter life lame, rather than having two feet, to be cast into hell, into the fire that shall never be quenched–where 'Their worm does not die, And the fire is not quenched.' And if your eye causes you to sin, pluck it out. It is better for you to enter the kingdom of God with one eye, rather than having two eyes, to be cast into hell fire–where 'Their worm does not die, And the fire is not quenched.'"
– Mark 9:43-48 NKJV

Though Christ may be referring to Hell here and not the Lake of Fire, one thing is certain: the consequences are real, and the punishment is fierce and continual! Jesus is using a phrase of speech called "hyperbole" to get the attention of His listeners regarding sin in their lives. He uses the exaggerated imagery of amputating a body part that causes you to sin, as a better option than keeping it and being cast into the fires of eternal punishment!

As He usually did, Jesus is quoting from the Old Testament. This passage is taken from the end of the book of Isaiah where he states:

"For as the new heavens and the new earth which I will make shall remain before Me," says the LORD, "So shall your descendants and your name remain. And it shall come to pass that from one New Moon to another, and from one Sabbath to another, all flesh shall come to worship before Me," says the LORD. "And they shall go forth and look upon the corpses of the men who have transgressed against Me. For their worm does not die, and their fire is not quenched. They shall be an abhorrence to all flesh."
– Isaiah 66:22-24 NKJV

This is not a symbolic or allegorical passage. The Bible should always be taken literally unless there are strong reasons for doing otherwise. It's well been said that *"..if the plain sense of a scripture makes sense, then seek no other sense!"* This is clearly a passage where Isaiah is looking into the future and speaking of the end of the Millennial Kingdom. He describes a real event of adoration that will take place, but also the gazing upon of people who have rebelled and transgressed against the Lord, as they are punished for their sin, in flames of wrath!

Will The Lake Of Fire Be Physical Torment?

As we said earlier, there are many groups and individuals today that don't believe in the eternal punishment of the wicked. Jehovah Witnesses, Hindus, Buddhists, Atheists, along with well known individuals like Rob Bell, Oprah, and Shirley Temple, are examples of this. However, the Scriptures clearly teach that even unbelievers and the unrighteous will receive resurrection bodies in eternity. Jesus put it like this in John's Gospel:

"Most assuredly, I say to you, the hour is coming, and now is, when the dead will hear the voice of the Son of God; and those who hear will live. For as the Father has life in Himself, so He has granted the Son to have life in Himself, and has given Him authority to execute judgment also, because He is the Son of Man. Do not marvel at this; for the hour is coming in which all who are in the graves will hear His voice and come forth– those who have done good, to the resurrection of life, and those who have done evil, to the resurrection of condemnation."
– John 5:24-29 NKJV

As Jesus made very clear, it's not only the redeemed and that will receive resurrected bodies in the Kingdom of Heaven. He clearly taught that even the unsaved will be given immortal bodies that will never die. For what purpose? To be able to physically endure the just punishment for their sins and rejection of Jesus! These immortal bodies which they'll receive, will never be destroyed, thus allowing them to be tormented for all eternity for their wickedness. These are the eternal ramifications of rejecting Christ and His forgiveness!

This should cause each of us to pause and reflect on the seriousness of sin, and the terrible consequences in store for those who refuse to repent and turn to Jesus Christ for forgiveness. The Scriptures teach us that the just punishment for sin is death (Romans 6:23), and that the soul that sins shall die and be separated from God eternally (Ezekiel 18:20). If GOD is truly *good* and perfect, then He *must* punish evil and wickedness. Therefore, since God *is* perfect and good, Hell and the Lake of Fire are a *necessity*. Since He is perfect, the eternal punishment of the wicked must take place...as described here in Revelation 20.

What Will The Final Judgement Be Like?

To end our discussion of Revelation 20 and the Millennium, let's discuss what the Great White Throne Judgement will be like. Let's examine the words of John as he describes it:

"Then I saw a great white throne and Him who sat on it, from whose face the earth and the heaven fled away. And there was found no place for them. And I saw the dead, small and great, standing before God, and books were opened. And another book was opened, which is the Book of Life. And the dead were judged according to their works, by the things which were written in the books. The sea gave up the dead who were in it, and Death and Hades delivered up the dead who were in them. And they were judged, each

one according to his works. Then Death and Hades were cast into the lake of fire. This is the second death. And anyone not found written in the Book of Life was cast into the lake of fire."
– Revelation 20:11-15 NKJV

As John describes this last event of the Millennium, we can see how this Judgement will transpire, who will appear there, and what the principle of this "Heavenly Courtroom" will be guided by. We'll examine this Final Judgement from 3 different angles: its *People*, its *Potentate*, and its *Principle*.

#1- The PEOPLE in the Final Judgement

John tells us that this Judgement is not for the saved, or the angels, but rather for the unrighteous dead of all the ages. We know this because it tells us that the "sea", "death", and "Hades" will give up the souls of the dead that are in them, and that this group will be composed of humans that were "small and great" during their lifetimes. This group of people are the unsaved humans throughout all of history, that have chosen to reject the One True GOD and the Savior Jesus Christ, and to live for sin and self. This is the moment when all souls of the unredeemed will appear in resurrected bodies before the Great White Throne, to hear the verdict from the Judge of the Universe regarding their sin and rebellion! (Read John 3:16-18; 14:6)

#2–The POTENTATE of the Final Judgement

John also describes the Potentate and Ruler who is conducting these "Heavenly Court Proceedings". It is none other than God Himself, sitting upon the Throne, judging unrighteous humanity. The Throne is described as being *"great"* and *"white"*, referring to the God's Almighty power and His perfect Holiness of character. It's for these reasons that He is able to sit in Judgement over all of humanity. The greatness mentioned here, speaks of the fact that He is the Almighty Creator. All belongs to Him because of the simple fact that He created it. Since God has created all good things, and owns all in the universe, He has the right to pass everlasting judgement over the destiny of every person. Because He is our Creator, He is qualified to be our Judge!

But this right is also His because of His purity and perfection, spoken of by the whiteness of the Throne. The Triune GOD–Father, Son, and Spirit,–is the only One in all of Creation that is completely perfect in all His ways, absolutely Holy, and completely separate from sin or moral weakness. It is *impossible* for the Lord to ever fail, sin, or do anything less than perfect! His Holy character is the very definition of "good" in the universe. Goodness flows from the heart and Person of GOD, as light and heat pour from the sun. As He is the Perfect and Holy One, He alone possesses the right to sit upon the Great White Throne and pass judgment upon humanity!

#3–The PRINCIPLE for the Final Judgement

The last component of this Judgement is the principle upon which it is based: *the sinful condition of the
people before the Throne!* As John's describes it here,
the people appearing at this judgement will be eval-
uated by "the books" that were opened, and by one
book in particular, the "Book of Life". While we don't
know exactly what these books are, or specifically
what they contain, one thing is for certain: knowing
Jesus as Savior is the final and ultimate criteria for
a person's salvation! The only way to gain entrance
into Heaven is by knowing the King Himself!

We know this, because it's taught throughout the
pages of Scripture. Peter tells us that Jesus is the only
name which can save a person (Acts 4:12). Paul says
if you declare that "Jesus is the Lord" and believe
that He is risen from the dead, then you can be saved
(Romans 10:9). Timothy was told that there is only
one Mediator between God and Man, the Man Christ
Jesus (1Tim 2:4). Jesus Himself clearly taught that
He was the only Way, Truth, and Life that leads to
the Father in Heaven (John 14:6).

However, without Jesus as their sacrifice for sin,
every single person that appears before the Great
White Throne Judgement will fail it miserably. Since
this Judgement depends on a person's relationship
to Christ as Lord and Savior, not a single person at
this Judgement will pass it! All of these will face the
horrible, but just and fair recompense, of paying for
their sins and rejection of the Son of God – Jesus
Christ. Their punishment is an eternal one, and it
will be forever paid in the Lake of Fire. This is the

tragic, but just fate, of all those who die without knowing Christ as Lord and Savior, rejecting His free offer of forgiveness and grace.

This brings us now to the 3rd and final phase of God's Heavenly Plan: the New Heavens and New Earth!

Chapter 4

Phase #3: The Eternal Heavens

As we have examined the Scriptures, we've seen that the 1st Phase of God's Eternal plan is the *"Dimension of Heaven"*, where believers will stand before the Throne of God, worship with the angels and saints of the ages, and receive crowns and rewards for their faithful service to Christ.

Next, we learned that when Jesus returns to the earth in the Second Coming, He will usher in the 2nd Phase of God's plan, the *"Kingdom of Heaven"*, called the Millennium, which will last for 1,000 years upon the earth. During this time, Jesus will rule from the capital city of Jerusalem, satan will bound and incarcerated, the saints will reign with Christ over the planet, nature will be greatly restored and renewed, long life spans will return to humanity, and it will end with a gigantic battle surrounding Jerusalem leading into the Great White Throne Judgement. All of these elements will transpire during this 2nd Phase of God's plan for Heaven.

But finally, after thousands of years of patiently waiting and earnestly longing, the last and final phase of God's plan will be ushered in upon the cosmos: ***the "Eternal Heavens".*** This is the glorious climax and the wonderful finale of the plan of God for the ages. This 3rd Phase of Heaven, is the dream that we've been longing for, and the answer we've been praying for, since the beginning of the Church!

One of the best places to which we can turn for information regarding this final stage of Heaven are the last two chapters of the Bible. Let's begin by examining a portion of what Revelation 21 tells us about the Eternal Heavens. John describes it like this:

"Now I saw a new heaven and a new earth, for the first heaven and the first earth had passed away. Also there was no more sea. Then I, John, saw the holy city, New Jerusalem, coming down out of heaven from God, prepared as a bride adorned for her husband. And I heard a loud voice from heaven saying, "Behold, the tabernacle of God is with men, and He will dwell with them, and they shall be His people. God Himself will be with them and be their God." And God will wipe away every tear from their eyes; there shall be no more death, nor sorrow, nor crying. There shall be no more pain, for the former things have passed away." Then He who sat on the throne said, "Behold, I make all things new." And He said to me, "Write, for these words are true and faithful." And He said to me, "It is done! I am the Alpha and the Omega, the Beginning and the End. I will give of the fountain of the

water of life freely to him who thirsts. "He who overcomes shall inherit all things, and I will be his God and he shall be My son. "But the cowardly, unbelieving, abominable, murderers, sexually immoral, sorcerers, idolaters, and all liars shall have their part in the lake which burns with fire and brimstone, which is the second death."
– Revelation 21:1-8 NKJV

What Will Be "New" In The New Heavens & New Earth?

This is a very good question and the answer is very simple: *Everything!* The Lord declares that He will *"make all things new"* (Revelation 21:5) during this 3rd Phase of Heaven. The word that is used here by John for *"new"* is the Greek word **"kainós"** which means *"something completely new, unprecedented; a brand new and fresh variety."* **"Kainos"** does not mean something old that has been polished up and made clean. Rather, this word refers to something that has never yet been seen; something completely fresh, unique, and of a brand new variety. That is what the Eternal Heavens will be like – a brand new earth, that has never been seen before, along with a brand new cosmos!

John tells us that one of the "new" features will be the earth itself, recreated in its entirety! Peter the apostle also speaks of this event in the distant future. He puts it like this:

"But the day of the Lord will come as a thief in the night, in which the heavens will pass away with a great noise, and the elements will melt

with fervent heat; both the earth and the works that are in it will be burned up. Therefore, since all these things will be dissolved, what manner of persons ought you to be in holy conduct and godliness, looking for and hastening the coming of the day of God, because of which the heavens will be dissolved, being on fire, and the elements will melt with fervent heat? Nevertheless we, according to His promise, look for new heavens and a new earth in which righteousness dwells."
– 2 Peter 3:10-13 NKJV

As Peter describes it, the elements themselves will melt with tremendous heat, the earth will be burned up and dissolved, and all of this will happen with great noise as it passes away. Not surprisingly, many bible teachers see in these words a striking similarity to the effects of atomic fission in a nuclear explosion!

Peter declares that the future destruction and renewal of the earth should practically affect Christians lives today. He says that since this world is only temporary, we should live in holiness and not grow too attached to it, as we anxiously await the New Heavens and New Earth.

This is what John means when he states that "the first heavens and the first earth had passed away". The Lord will melt and dissolve them at some point in the future, reconstitute the planet and the entire universe into a brand new and fresh Creation. What a glorious day that will be: new planets, new stars, new galaxies and solar systems for us to explore, enjoy, and serve the Lord in!

Not only will there be a new earth, in a brand new universe, but there will also be a new difference on our planet: there will be no more sea! Even though they will be present during the Millennial Kingdom, in this 3rd phase of God's Heavenly plan, the need for oceans and seas will be a thing of the past.

Though this has often been the cause of great sadness and confusion for Christian surfers and beach enthusiasts, it seems to be the plain understanding of these verses. This means that there will probably have to be a "new" kind of ecological system and process regulating the New Earth, as the current one depends so heavily on the presence of the seas and oceans. Enjoy the oceans while you can during the Millennium, because they will be a thing of the past in the Eternal Heavens (at least on planet earth)!

Interestingly, after writing dozens of chapters regarding the Kingdom of Heaven, in chapter 65, Isaiah the prophet turns his attention towards the Eternal Heavens, making a striking statement:

> **"For behold, I create new heavens and a new earth; And the former shall not be remembered or come to mind."**
> **– Isaiah 65:17 NKJV**

It seems that there will be an aspect of our life in the New Heavens and New Earth, in which we won't be "missing" or "longing" after this current world, but will rather simply be enjoying and exploring all the new features the Lord will have created. Eventually, the old earth and old universe will gradually fade from our minds, and I believe, not be remembered by us anymore. This is a beautiful act of mercy on the part of God, as this sin-filled and misery-ridden world, will no longer depress or distress us, as it simply fades from our memory in the Eternal Heavens!

Other "new" features of the Eternal Heavens, will include the new dwelling place of the saints, along with the new state of perfection that will prevail on earth and throughout the cosmos. Let's examine each of these in turn.

What Will The "Eternal Heavens" Be Like?

Another "new" feature of this 3rd and final phase, will be the dwelling place of the saints. The apostle John declares there will be a magnificent city where glorified believers will live during this period–the New Jerusalem! He writes this:

"Then I, John, saw the holy city, New Jerusalem, coming down out of heaven from God, prepared as a bride adorned for her husband. And I heard a loud voice from heaven saying, "Behold, the tabernacle of God is with men, and He will dwell with them, and they shall be His people. God Himself will be with them and be their God."
– Revelation 21:2-3 NKJV

Many believers are unaware that one of the main descriptions of the Eternal Heavens, is that of a perfect celestial city. This is interesting, since most humans think of "getting away" to the beach or mountains for a time of enjoyment and relaxation. However, God made us to exist in relationship with Himself and other people, and it will be fully embodied when this heavenly metropolis appears.

This glorious city of "New Jerusalem" will be the dwelling place of the redeemed in eternity, and will serve as the New Capital of the New Earth. It is described here as the "tabernacle of God" which is a way to speak of His personal presence abiding with mankind in a visible, tangible form. Just think of it: seeing the LORD face to Face, and physically dwelling with Him for all of eternity, in this perfect city and His newly created universe! Surely, this will be the true joy and adventure of eternity! John continues to describe the city in Revelation's last chapter, where he says:

"... the throne of God and of the Lamb shall be in it, and His servants shall serve Him. They shall see His face, and His name shall be on their foreheads. There shall be no night there: They need no lamp nor light of the sun, for the Lord God gives them light. And they shall reign forever and ever."
– Revelation 22:3-5 NKJV

It's further described as *"a bride"* who is adorned and made ready for her Husband. This is obviously a description of the Bride of Christ, the Church, as we will be the ones inhabiting and living in New Jerusalem. John's Gospel (Jn 3:29) also refers to the Church as *"the bride"* and Jesus as our *"bridegroom"* who will come and receive us to Himself. As this chapter continues, John speaks further of the

Bride and the city of New Jerusalem, her eternal dwelling place:

"Then one of the seven angels who had the seven bowls filled with the seven last plagues came to me and talked with me, saying, "Come, I will show you the bride, the Lamb's wife." And he carried me away in the Spirit to a great and high mountain, and showed me the great city, the holy Jerusalem, descending out of heaven from God, having the glory of God. Her light was like a most precious stone, like a jasper stone, clear as crystal. Also she had a great and high wall with twelve gates, and twelve angels at the gates, and names written on them, which are the names of the twelve tribes of the children of Israel: three gates on the east, three gates on the north, three gates on the south, and three gates on the west. Now the wall of the city had twelve foundations, and on them were the names of the twelve apostles of the Lamb."
– Revelation 21:9-14 NKJV

We see that the city of New Jerusalem is "great" and "holy", speaking of its magnitude and its purity. It will be the greatest city ever inhabited by human beings, and it will be one that is absolutely perfect, completely free of any sinful presence or activity. It's also described as having the "glory of God" within it. This may refer to the *"Shekinah"* glory of the Old Testament, a visible representation of God's presence, that filled the Tabernacle in the "Holy of Holies" as described in Exodus 40:34-35.

John further describes the city as having a high wall surrounding it, twelve gates (3 on each side), mighty angels at each gate, and twelve huge foundations. He tells us that each of the foundations is inscribed with one of the names of the twelve apostles, and that each gate is inscribed with the names of the tribes of Israel. This is fitting, as the apostles' teaching and the Jewish scriptures form the spiritual foundation and "entrance" through which we pass, to come into Christ's Kingdom! (Read John 10:7-9)

Based on this description, it's obvious to see that this is describing a *literal* and *physical* city that will actually exist in our universe. I say this, because there are certain Bible teachers and Christian groups who seek to *"spiritualize"* and *"allegorize"* the book of Revelation, such as Calvinists, Reformed, and other *"Amillennial"* believers. The very fact that these precise details are given, clearly shows this is meant to be taken literally, at face value, and that this is a real city being seen and described by John.

The *"Golden Rule"* of all Bible interpretation is to always take the Bible literally (according to its genre) and straightforward, unless there is clear direction and reason for doing otherwise. To not do this creates the danger of false doctrine, false teaching, or even heresy, in the life of a church or an individual Christian. As mentioned earlier, if the *plain sense* of the text *makes sense*... seek no *other sense!*

We have further reason to believe this is a real, literal city, as John continues to give us detailed measurements and the specific size of New Jerusalem:

"And he who talked with me had a gold reed to measure the city, its gates, and its wall. The city is laid out as a square; its length is as great as its breadth. And he measured the city with the reed: twelve thousand furlongs. Its length, breadth, and height are equal. Then he measured its wall: one hundred and forty-four cubits, according to the measure of a man, that is, of an angel. The construction of its wall was of jasper; and the city was pure gold, like clear glass."
– Revelation 21:15-18 NKJV

First, we see that the city of New Jerusalem will be constructed as a gigantic and perfect cube! John tells us that its length, width, and breadth are all the same. He tells us that the city measures "12,000 furlongs" on each of its sides. This is an old measurement, but we can calculate the size using modern conversions:

1 furlong = .125 miles

If we simply multiply this by 12,000 we get the length of each side of New Jerusalem:

Length of New Jerusalem:
12,000 x .125 miles = 1,500 miles

Distance from New York City to Denver, Colorado:
1,493 miles

Each side of this cubed Heavenly City will be 1,500 miles long, about the distance from the city of New York City to Denver, Colorado; or the distance from Los Angeles to Minneapolis, Minnesota! This city of New Jerusalem will almost stretch across the length of the United States of America – incredible!

However, don't forget that it's also a staggering 1,500 miles high into the atmosphere! How can we envision this height in our mind's eye? Well, consider the fact that the highest mountains on earth are only about 5 miles tall, and that commercial airliners normally fly at around 6 miles high.

In contrast to this, the New Jerusalem will rise 1,500 miles into the air, which is well beyond Earth's present atmosphere. The entire atmosphere of our planet only reaches about 300 miles at its maximum, which means that the New Jerusalem will be bulging out 1,200 miles beyond the limits of the ozone, into outer space! Envision yourself standing on the top of this mammoth structure and looking down on the earth below from this City – what a breathtaking view it will be!

This also means, that if New Jerusalem were to have 12 feet per story in its structure, as most buildings do today, this Heavenly City would rise 600,000 stories high, breaking through the atmosphere into outer space! Imagine the sight of this enormous structure if you were standing at ground level, and then peered up vertically to see its massive sides rise into the sky! It will be a monolith of heavenly architecture to gaze upon for all of humanity!

The Cubic Volume of New Jerusalem:
1,500 miles x 1,500 miles x 1,500 miles =
3,375,000,000 cubic miles

The massive dimensions of New Jerusalem work out to be a total volume of over 3.3 billion cubic miles in volume. This is a greater volume than that of the moon! With today's population of about 7 billion, each person on earth would be able to have a "mansion" in this city that would be about .5 miles long, wide, and high. It will truly be an enormously massive structure!

What about the diameter of New Jerusalem? It calculates out to be well over 2,400 miles! For the sake of reference, the diameter of the moon is only 2,160 miles. This means that the Heavenly City will be even larger than our current moon orbiting the earth, in the night sky!

Because of its enormous size, many physicists believe that the Law of Gravity may not affect New Jerusalem in the way it does objects today. Since anything with a diameter of over 300 km naturally collapses into the shape of a sphere, this apparently won't be the case for the Heavenly City, which maintains the shape of a perfect cube.

This is interesting, since the "Holy of Holies" in the Old Testament Tabernacle was *also* a perfect cube in its dimensions: 10 x 10 x 10 cubits. (Read Exodus 25-26) This is very significant, since the "Holy of Holies" was where the LORD met Moses face to face, and spoke with him in intimate communion. In the New Jerusalem, we too will see the LORD face to face, speak with Him intimately, and serve Him faithfully ... for all of eternity! (Read Revelation 22:4)

What Will New Jerusalem Look Like?

Aside from its sheer size and massive volume, we're also told of certain external features of the city, and even of the building materials used for the construction of New Jerusalem.

First, John describes for us that the city has a wall that is 144 cubits high. Interesting, since 12 x 12 equals 144, and 12 is an important number in the Bible (12 tribes, 12 apostles, 12 gates, 12 foundations). With a little calculation, we can figure out how high this wall will be in modern measurements:

Height of the Wall of New Jerusalem (short cubit):
1 cubit = 17.5 inches
144 cubits = 2,520 inches = 210 feet high

Height of the Wall of New Jerusalem (long cubit):
1 cubit = 20.4 inches
144 cubits = 2,937.6 inches = 244.8 feet high

Depending on if we use the "short" or the "long" measurement for an ancient cubit, we discover that the wall surrounding New Jerusalem will be somewhere between 210 feet high, or about 245 feet high. Either way, the impressive wall surrounding this massive City will be over 20 stories high!

Furthermore, John tells us it will be constructed out of jasper stone, which has a deep reddish color.

This is due to high amounts of iron inside jasper. It's also closely related to another type of rock called a "bloodstone", both of which were worn by Christians in the early church, as a reminder of Christ's sacrifice upon the cross. Jasper is also mentioned as the twelfth and last stone on the breastplate of the High Priest in the Old Testament in Exodus 28:20.

It seems then, that the wall of New Jerusalem will be deep reddish in color. As such, this massive structure will remind us for all eternity that it is the Blood of the Lamb, that protects us and shields us, from sin and destruction. For countless future ages, the saints will gaze upon the wall of this city, as an immoveable testimony and permanent reminder of the sacrifice of the King, on their behalf! (Read John 15:13)

A Heavenly City Of Pure Gold!

We are told that the city itself will be constructed of pure gold, as clear as glass. Gold, in the ancient world, was understood to be the metal of kings and royalty, and today is still one of the most valuable substances on earth. How fitting then, that the New Jerusalem would be built out of it, as the Great King will dwell there, and the saints will rule at His side, as lesser kings and queens throughout all of eternity!

It's interesting that John describes the gold being as clear as glass. Though he may have seen something completely different, with modern technology, we have the ability to create ultra-thin and transparent sheets of gold. Thin gold sheets display some unusual characteristics. When processed in ultra-thin sheets, gold becomes transparent. It allows green light waves to pass through, while reflecting infrared light. Windows coated with gold allow light to enter, but all the while reflecting heat. Therefore, many cockpit windows of modern aircraft are coated with gold, as well as the windows of office buildings, in order to take advantage of these unique properties.

Whatever the case, we know that this Heavenly City will be one that is made of pure gold, as clear as glass, allowing the glory of the light of God to shine through it; it will tower up through our atmosphere, extending 1,200 miles out into space; it will have 3 gates on the north, south, east, and west; and it will be surrounded by a wall over 20 stories high, made of red jasper to remind us of the blood sacrifice of our great God and King!

Next, John describes the foundation of the New Jerusalem, focusing on the types of stones it will constructed of. He wrote this:

"The foundations of the wall of the city were adorned with all kinds of precious stones: the first foundation was jasper, the second sapphire, the third chalcedony, the fourth emerald, the fifth sardonyx, the sixth sardius, the seventh chrysolite, the eighth beryl, the ninth topaz, the tenth chrysoprase, the eleventh jacinth, and the twelfth amethyst. The twelve gates were twelve pearls: each individual gate was of one pearl. And the street of the city was pure gold, like transparent glass. But I saw no temple in it, for the Lord God Almighty and the Lamb are its temple. The city had no need of the sun or of the moon to shine in it, for the glory of God

illuminated it. The Lamb is its light."
– Revelation 21:19-23 NKJV

The foundation of the Heavenly Capital will be marvelously colored with these 12 beautiful stones, as described by John. There is a strong connection between these "Foundation Stones" and the 12 stones of the High Priest's breastplate, as described in Exodus 25-26. Much could be gleaned from these verses, by examining and comparing the stone types and their individual meaning. We won't take the time to do it here, but I would encourage you to do so, in your own personal study. (Read 2 Timothy 2:15)

Are There "Pearly Gates" In New Jerusalem?

John tells us that each of the gates in New Jerusalem will be made of a single, enormous pearl! I'm sure that the beauty of these gates, and their immense size, will be a wonderful sight to behold, as we enter the Heavenly Capital for the first time!

Many Bible teachers find meaning in the fact that, not only are pearls extremely valuable, but they're also made through an interesting process. When a small irritant (such as a pebble or grain of sand) becomes lodged inside of an oyster, it's coated again and again with a special chemical called "nacre", also known as "mother of pearl". This object is then rounded continually inside the oyster through rubbing against the inner shell. Eventually, this elaborate process produces a precious and beautiful pearl, often of gem-like quality.

In a very real sense, the oyster takes something negative, irritating, and painful, and turns it into something positive, lovely, and valuable. This is a beautiful metaphor of how the Lord will use trials, suffering, and pain in the life of every believer, and ultimately turn it into something good and beneficial, when they arrive in Heaven. Scripture promises that all of our experiences and situations in this life, no matter how difficult or painful, will ultimately be turned into a thing of beauty and joy, by the time we enter the pearly gates of New Jerusalem! (Read Romans 8:28; Genesis 50:20)

No Temple In The Heavenly City?!?

John mentions that there is one architectural feature curiously absent from the Heavenly City: a Temple. This famous building that has served as the cultural and spiritual center of Israel for so long, even during the Millennium, will be curiously absent in the Eternal Heavens and the New Jerusalem. Why? It seems that the original purpose of the Temple will finally see its ultimate fulfillment: GOD Himself will live and abide in the midst of His people... in visible form!

The Temple always represented the desire of the LORD to dwell in the midst of His people, being the center of their national life, but also the nucleus of each person's spiritual life. Though this was never truly the case due to sin, in New Jerusalem and the Eternal Heavens, it will finally be realized. The LORD will meet with His people on a personal basis, for communion and intimate fellowship! His presence will even illuminate and shine throughout the city of New Jerusalem, making the light of the sun unnecessary, though it will likely still exist. What a glorious and wonderful life it will be in the Eternal Heavens, dwelling in this paradise of New Jerusalem!

Will There Be Different Nations on the New Earth?

John also describes some of the special people that will visit New Jerusalem in this 3rd and final phase of God's plan for the ages. He puts it like this:

"And the nations of those who are saved shall walk in its light, and the kings of the earth bring their glory and honor into it. Its gates shall not be shut at all by day (there shall be no night there). And they shall bring the glory and the honor of the nations into it. But there shall by no means enter it anything that defiles, or causes an abomination or a lie, but only those who are written in the Lamb's Book of Life."
– Revelation 21:24-27 NKJV

Here we see that the governing royalty and kings from the New Earth will regularly bring homage and gifts of worship into the City to be given to the Great King. As we've previously discussed, these kings will be the redeemed and glorified saints, who received these positions of authority during the Judgment Seat of Christ. These are the kings who will enter the New Jerusalem to offer gifts of thanksgiving and worship to King Jesus. They will represent the individual nations they govern on the New Earth.

This emphasizes an interesting and important feature of the Eternal Heavens. First, there will be distinct countries and "nations", each with a king ruling over them, in service to Christ. It's helpful to remember that originally, human government was the second institution created by the Lord (Genesis 9:6), as a blessing for all humanity, and a representation of His care and protection. Though this is often not the case in today's sin torn world, it was the original design in the heart of God.

However, this will climax into its perfect and final form in the Eternal Heavens, as glorified humans, will exercise a sinless and holy rule over the earth, and it's sinless and holy people, carrying out the wishes and policies of their Great King. It will be the ultimate fulfillment of God's original plans for government on earth: a Theocracy in which He rules over us in His love, grace, and righteousness, and we respond in sinless, loving obedience!

Next, there are distinct "nations" mentioned by John, meaning a plurality of different countries will exist on the New Earth. This is important, as you picture and envision the world of the Eternal Heavens, and what it will be like for us practically. There will be different cultures, people groups, national boundaries, and perhaps even languages in these nations of the New Earth. Much like in the Millennium, the New Earth will be a literal and physical place, where perfected and sinless humans will live under the reign of Jesus, all the while inhabiting glorious cities, serving in heavenly ministries, and engaging in a wonderful culture of holy worshippers!

The New Heavens and New Earth will be very similar to the Millennial Kingdom in terms of function and organization, but will be distinct in that they will finally exist in a *__perfected__* and *__sinless__* state, as it was always meant to. Remember what we learned:

"Heaven is coming to Earth!" and this is the ultimate fulfillment of it!

New Jerusalem – A Paradise Garden City!

In the final chapter of Revelation, John describes the inside of New Jerusalem, and some of the features that we'll see, as we enter through its gates of pearl. He describes it with these colorful words:

"And he showed me a pure river of water of life, clear as crystal, proceeding from the throne of God and of the Lamb. In the middle of its street, and on either side of the river, was the tree of life, which bore twelve fruits, each tree yielding its fruit every month. The leaves of the tree were for the healing of the nations."
– Revelation 22:1-2 NKJV

Based on this description and other verses in Scripture, many Bible teachers believe that this paradise of New Jerusalem will resemble a kind of "Garden City" as you enter its gates and behold your surroundings.

First, John describes a "pure river of water of life" that comes from the Throne of God and the Lamb. This will be a real, literal river, clear as crystal that flows throughout the City of New Jerusalem. It will likely create an atmosphere of peace, tranquility, and refreshment for all those who are near it. I say this, because if you've ever walked through a city (such as San Antonio) with a mighty and beautiful river flowing through the middle of it, you know the peaceful influence this can have on the soul of its citizens. It's a simple but powerful effect! However, this is no ordinary river. Rather, it's a "River of Life" which is sure to have unique properties that will refresh and revitalize all who bask in its crystal clear waters!

The Tree Of Life–In New Jerusalem?!?

John also depicts a special Tree that will find its ultimate resting place within the walls of this Garden City: the Tree of Life! This infamous tree was first mentioned in the Garden of Eden, when the Lord commanded that sinful man couldn't be allowed to eat from it. Many Bible teachers believe that if Adam had done so, humans would have going on living forever, in sinful decaying bodies, as immortals. It was a pure act of loving mercy and grace that the Lord ejected Adam and Eve from the Garden before this could happen! (Read Genesis 3:22-24)

However, here we see that the Tree of Life is "transplanted" and moved into the New Jerusalem, to be enjoyed by all of glorified humanity, for all time! This Tree of Life, will grow on both sides of the River of Life, in the middle, and probably throughout different portions of the City as well. Incredibly, even though Adam and Eve weren't allowed to eat from this Tree, you'll be able to see it, touch it, and be nourished by it, in the Heavenly Paradise of New Jerusalem!

Eating Fruit In New Jerusalem?!?

John paints a colorful picture of this Tree by describing the kind of fruit that will grow on it for the people of New Jerusalem. Imagine how delicious and wonderful the fruit will taste from a Tree that grows in the Heavenly City, is nourished by the River of Life, and was created by the hand of God Himself! It will be the most delicious fruit ever tasted by man, to be sure!

He also tells us also that this Tree will grow 12 different kinds of fruits, a different one for each month of the year. Not only will this be the most delicious fruit ever grown, but it will be a different kind every month. Just imagine, one month it might be mouthwatering mangos; the next month succulent strawberries; the next month heavenly apples... it will be delightful and delicious!

Not only will we eat in our glorified resurrected bodies in the Millennial Kingdom, but we'll continue to do so on into the Eternal Heavens, as we inhabit the New Jerusalem and rule over the New Earth. The menu will quite literally be "out of this world!"

<u>Heavenly "Therapy" In New Jerusalem?!?</u>

Notice that John tells us two more interesting details: the leaves of the Tree will be therapeutic in nature, and we will still follow a monthly calendar in the Eternal Heavens.

The word for *"healing"* that is used is the Greek word *"therapeia"* from which we derive the English word *"therapy"*. It's a word that speaks of healing and medicinal benefit. Although there will be no sickness in the Eternal Heavens, the leaves of this Tree will aid us in a therapeutic sense by strengthening, revitalizing, and physically empowering our glorified resurrection bodies, to an even greater degree!

Will Time Exist In The New Heavens And New Earth?

According to this passage in Revelation 22, the New Earth and New Jerusalem will still be using some sort of monthly calendar. John said that "every month" the fruit of this Tree will change. I mentions this, simply to highlight the fact that Scripture teaches us that humans will continue to live *in time* on the New Earth, as we do on this Earth. Just like fish need water to live in, humans need time to exist in, and this will never change, even in the Eternal Heavens. I've heard many Bible teachers and Christians say that *"time won't exist anymore"* or that in Heaven *"we'll step out of time and into timeless eternity",* which simply isn't the case according to Scripture.

Not only are there huge metaphysical problems with those statements, they just happen to simply be against what the Bible teaches regarding Heaven. For and in-depth philosophical treatment of this, read the book *"Time and Eternity: Exploring God's Relationship to Time"* by Dr. William Lane Craig, one of the finest Christian thinkers of our time. He's a deep thinker, so strap on your "thinking cap"!

Ever since Genesis 1:1 when the Lord called all time, space, matter, and energy into being, our physical universe has functioned with time as a major component. This will continue on into the eternal future, as we serve and love the LORD forever and ever, time without end!

Will The "Eternal Heavens" Be Truly Perfect?

A final question that arises in our minds about Heaven, and this phase of God's plan for the ages, is whether things will ever truly be in a state of sinless perfection. The loud and clear answer of Scripture is *"YES!"* In the last chapter of Revelation, John expresses it with these beautiful words:

> *"And there shall be no more curse,*
> *but the throne of God and of the Lamb shall be in*
> *it, and His servants shall serve Him."*
> *– Revelation 22:3 NKJV*

In biblical terminology, John told us that the New Heavens and New Earth will exist in a state of perfection, since "the curse" will no longer be present in our universe. The "curse" referred to here is the sin, death, and decay that entered the human race and the world, when Adam sinned in the Garden of Eden (Read Genesis 3). Paul the apostle comments on this in Romans 5, when speaking of Adam's fall with these words:

> *"Therefore, just as through one man sin entered*
> *the world, and death through sin, and thus*
> *death spread to all men..."*
> *– Romans 5:12 NKJV*

This was the beginning of the "curse", as Adam willfully disobeyed his Creator, followed his own will, and committed the first sin of the human race. This is where Scripture tells us that death and the decaying effect we now see operating in the universe, entered into God's creation. In Genesis 3 we read this account:

"Then to Adam He said, "Because you have heeded the voice of your wife, and have eaten from the tree of which I commanded you, saying, 'You shall not eat of it': "Cursed is the ground for your sake; In toil you shall eat of it all the days of your life. Both thorns and thistles it shall bring forth for you, and you shall eat the herb of the field. In the sweat of your face you shall eat bread till you return to the ground, for out of it you were taken; For dust you are, and to dust you shall return."
– Genesis 3:17-19 NKJV

This was the tragic moment when the "curse" of sin began to ravage the bodies of man, the planet earth, and the universe itself! Today, the deteriorating effect where things go from order to disorder, from organization to disorganization, or from high energy to low energy is called the "Law of Entropy" or the "Second Law of Thermodynamics". Regardless of what we call it from a scientific perspective, it seems that according to the Bible, it began with the sin of Adam, and has plagued us ever since. Ever since the Garden of Eden, the explosion of this "Adam Bomb" and the resulting "blast waves" of the curse, have been ravaging humanity and the earth in a very real way.

Based on what the Lord told Adam, the ground itself became cursed in this tragic moment. It would now require heavy and laborious work to bring forth a good harvest of food; thorns and thistles now appear in nature; and from this day forward, the human aging process began, ultimately ending in the physical death of the body. This is the dark heritage of the curse that humanity has inherited from Adam – deterioration, disease, and death! (Read Romans 6:23; Ezekiel 18:20)

However, God had different plans! The Lord always knew that Adam would sin, and had always planned from eternity to redeem fallen humanity, once He paid for sin and defeated satan by the Cross of Christ. The New Heavens and New Earth is the ultimate fulfillment of God's plan of the ages, which has been in His mind and heart forever!

John declared a beautiful promise that there will be "no more curse" in this final phase of Heaven. This will be the complete undoing and reversal of all that the curse has unleashed upon the human race. Everything will truly be made new and the entire universe will finally be brought into a state of sinless perfection! John described it with these comforting words:

"And God will wipe away every tear from their eyes; there shall be no more death, nor sorrow, nor crying. There shall be no more pain, for the former things have passed away." Then He who sat on the throne said, "Behold, I make all things new." And He said to me, "Write, for these words are true and faithful."
– Revelation 21:4-5 NKJV

This will be the day that we have so desperately longed for! We are told unequivocally that there will be no more death, no more sorrow, no more crying, and no more pain associated with sin. All of the bitter anguish and the sting of evil that has plagued humanity for thousands of years in wars, disease, and murder will exist no longer!

The Lord declares with utter finality that He will *"make all things new"* in this Eternal Heavens. The Greek word for ***"new"*** is the word ***"kainos"*** which means something completely new and different - a brand new variety. It's something that's totally fresh, and never seen before. The Lord is declaring, that in the Eternal Heavens He will create a new and fresh condition in our universe, one that has never been seen or experienced up to this point. It will be a condition of sinless perfection and everlasting peace!

This is the Heaven that people love to envision: one that is free from anything bad, painful, or evil like we see in our current world. This is the Heaven that all humanity longs for! Since the creation of mankind, the Lord has ***"put eternity in their hearts"*** (Ecclesiastes 3:11) which has produced a hunger and thirst for this state of perfection and heavenly bliss. Lest we think it's too good to be true, the book of Revelation ends with these words in the final chapter:

> ***"Then he said to me,***
> ***'These words are faithful and true.'"***
> ***– Revelation 22:6 NKJV***

Every false religion and empty philosophy of man, though confused and misled, ultimately desires this Heaven as its end goal. Whether it's the ***"Utopia"*** of Communism, the ***"Shangri La"*** of Hinduism, or the ***"Nirvana"*** of Buddhism, this is the day that all of mankind has been dreaming of since our beginnings in the Garden of Eden. But it can only be attained through the Lord Jesus Christ, and the forgiveness of sin He offers us through the Cross of Calvary. (Read John 14:6; Acts 4:12)

Finally, after thousands of years of cosmic conflict, waging a war on satan, sin, and the system of this world, the Lord Himself will usher in this time of refreshing and perfection, in which He will "make all things new" in this 3rd and final phase, the Eternal Heavens.

From this point of history onward, we will live forever in this New Heavens and New Earth, ruling and reigning at the side of Christ, from New Jerusalem. We will serve the Lord for all eternity, on this planet and beyond, in a newly created universe, full of unimaginable wonders and beauty! It will truly be a storybook ending, to the gruesome nightmare of human history. Here, in the Eternal Heavens, in the presence of the Father, Son, and Spirit, we will know a peace beyond description, a love beyond measure, and a purpose beyond imagination. For time without end, we will live *"happily ever after"* with our great God and King, in His Eternal Heavens!

Chapter 5

"Live For Heaven..Right Now!"

A well-known Bible teacher, Alexander Maclaren, once described how the reality of Heaven should affect our daily living:

> *"I do not know what we are in this world for, unless it is to apprentice us for Heaven. Life on earth is a bewilderment, unless we are being trained for a nobler work which lies beyond the grave."*

He's right. Biblically speaking, this life is a training ground for the Kingdom. This life is simply a type of "Pre-Season", to prepare us for the main event of Heaven on earth. This life is merely a "dress rehearsal", for the real "show" of the Kingdom that we're anxiously waiting for!

However, the million dollar question asked by every believer who truly wants to prepare for Heaven is this:

"How can I live for Heaven... right now?"

The answer is much simpler that you might think! You see, you've been given certain tools and resources by God. And do you know *why* He's given them to you? He hasn't done it in order to benefit you primarily. He's given them to you, so you can reinvest *His* resources, expand *His* Kingdom, and bring *other* people closer to Christ in the process!

Remember what Jesus told us in Matthew's Gospel about investing our lives in Heaven? He gave us this command:

"Do not lay up for yourselves treasures on earth, where moth and rust destroy and where thieves break in and steal; but lay up for yourselves treasures in heaven, where neither moth nor rust destroys and where thieves do not break in and steal. For where your treasure is, there your heart will be also."
– Matthew 6:20, 21 NKJV

First, Jesus told us what not to do–we're not to be storing up and accumulating treasures on earth right now. We're not to be living materialistically, focusing on the present world as our passion. Sadly, this is all too common today, isn't it? Even among Christians, many of us are captivated and seduced by the allures of materialism and the abundance of earthly riches. But Jesus clearly taught against this. If this world will eventually pass away in flames and be made anew, then it shouldn't be the focus of our major life investments. This was the point that Christ was making by speaking of "moth and rust" corrupting it, and "thieves" stealing it – it's all just temporary. Therefore, don't make this present world the focus of your ultimate passions and investments!

Next, Jesus instructed us what we _should_ be investing our resources in: *Heaven!* He wasn't being metaphorical or symbolic about this. If Jesus commands us to do something, it's obviously possible and practically doable. In other words, there are real and actual ways for Christians to store up and accumulate "treasures in Heaven". As we've learned by seeing the 3 Phases of God's eternal plan, Heaven is a real place, that's coming to earth, and Jesus wants us to send our treasures ahead, as an eternal investment!

By the way, did you notice what Jesus said would happen as a natural by-product when you "lay up treasures in Heaven"? Your heart becomes more attached _to_ Heaven, and longs more passionately _for_ Heaven! He said that wherever your treasures are invested, your heart will naturally follow. This is the great secret to developing a heart for Heaven: *Make considerable and consistent investments towards it, and your passion will grow even deeper for the Kingdom!*

But what exactly are these resources that you've received from Jesus? What are the tools and the resources He's given you to invest and expand the Kingdom of Heaven, right now? If we can discover what tools and talents the Lord has entrusted to us, then we can develop an effective strategy to _use_ them, _invest_ them, and _multiply_ them for the expansion of the Kingdom of Heaven...***right now!***

This is the topic we'll examine in this last chapter of our book – 4 major ways in which we can invest in Heaven, and live for Heaven...*today!*

Heavenly Investment #1:

My Time!

Time is the first precious resource you've been given by God. It's priceless, but also perishable, because it vanishes second-by-second of everyday! Every 24 hours the Lord gives you 86,400 seconds to use in an intelligent and diligent way for His Kingdom. Whether we choose to or not, at the end of that day, those precious 86,400 seconds can never be reclaimed or recaptured. They are simply gone... *forever!*

Once when I was traveling, I glanced into an in-flight shopping magazine and noticed a unique type of clock for sale. It was a digital clock, into which you could enter the day, the year, the time of your birth... and then press "enter". Based on the average human lifespan, this clock would then begin a reverse digital countdown of how much longer you have left to live!

What would *you* think if every time you got up in the morning, there it is – staring back at you, counting down to your death? If clocks aren't your thing, in our internet world and this "age of the app" there are plenty of desktop countdowns or apps that can achieve the same purpose. Many people have told me that they would never want such a device, since it would make them constantly think of their own mortality and lead them to pessimism or even depression.

However, I believe the Lord wants us to "keep an eye on the clock" of our life, in order to wisely use our time for His Kingdom. Moses actually prayed for this when he said these words, as recorded in the Psalms:

> *"We finish our years like a sigh. The days of our lives are seventy years; and if by reason of strength they are eighty years... For it is soon cut off, and we fly away... So teach us to number our days, that we may gain a heart of wisdom."*
> *– Psalm 90:9,10,12 NKJV*

Moses was asking the Lord to teach him to learn how to count down his remaining time on earth! Whether a person does this with a digital clock, an internet app, or by simply being aware of the use of their time, it's something that would be of great benefit to all of us, in living for Heaven more effectively!

Did you know that, in actuality, you already possess a clock like that? You have a clock just like that, floating above your head, ceaselessly counting down the seconds of your life! You can't see it visibly, but in a sense, it's there. You see, the Lord knows the years, months, weeks, days, and seconds you have left to live on this earth. This invisible "death clock" is always counting down for us, tick-tick-tick, but we just can't see it!

Time Is Chasing Us?!?

Do you remember the story of "Peter Pan" you learned as a child? One of the interesting characters depicted in that tale was the relentless crocodile that chased Captain Hook. Captain Hook wanted to know where the crocodile was at all times, because it had eaten his hand...which is precisely why they called him "Captain Hook". In order to keep better track of where the croc was at all times, Captain Hook somehow fed him a small clock! And so, in the books, in the movies, and in the cartoons, whenever Captain Hook hears the dreadful sound of, "Tick, tick, tick," he knows that the croc with the clock is on his scent again! He knows that the crocodile is right there, always *chasing* him, and relentlessly *pursuing* him!

In a very similar way, Time is chasing *you* too! It is constantly, relentlessly, mercilessly tracking *you* down as well! Time is chasing you and you're not going to escape it! You only have a limited time available in this short life, and it's counting down above your head, second by second. The question is simply this:

"How are you using the precious time God has given you?

How Big Is Your "Slice" Of Time?
  If you could envision the use of your daily time like a 3-dimensional pie graph, how big would the slice of time be for the category of entertainment? How about the time used for your hours of work? How big would the slice be for time spent sleeping? What about your recreation? For family time? For serving the Lord?

According to various statistics, the average human of 70 to 78 years of age today, will spend their time in the following ways (prepare to be shocked):

→ *25 years is spent working at your job.*
→ *25 years is spent sleeping in bed.*
→ *9 years used for eating food.*
→ *5 years doing miscellaneous things.*
→ *2 years waiting in traffic lights.*
→ *1 year spent tying your shoes.*
→ *3-8 years for personal pursuits.*

If these averages are correct, or even approximate, then you're only going to have about three to eight years to really give to God *entirely*. This works out to be somewhere between 26,280 hours to 70,080 hours that you'll have the chance to dedicate to the Lord and invest directly towards Heaven, in a meaningful way. Actually, that's quite a big chunk of time, if it's put to good use!

How To Use Your Time For Heaven

Here are some simple, but powerful suggestions I encourage you to consider and implement, in the daily and weekly use of your time. These simple changes to your schedule can truly help your life become an effective and serious investment in the Kingdom of Heaven!

#1 – Spend Time Reading Your Bible

Number one, we need to have a quiet time, with a quiet heart, in a quiet place reading God's Word and growing closer to Him in personal devotion. This is how we get to know the voice of our Master, and the truths of His Word. Only the Word of God can feed our spirits, and keep us strong and healthy before the Lord. If we nourish ourselves from it on a daily basis, we'll be full of vitality, power, and have the right perspective on the issues of life. This can happen by simply *reading* the Bible, *listening* to a teaching from a trusted teacher, or using a good *devotional book* on the Scriptures.

However, you choose to do this, it should be a time of undistracted focus upon the Word, in which you can deeply reflect on and think about what is being said. As you go thru the verses for that day, ask the Lord to show you how they apply to the situations going on in *your* life at that moment. Speak to Jesus and ask Him to apply His Word to your life *specifically*. Some people refer to this as "Prayer Reading" and others simply call it "meditation" (Psalm 1). Regardless of what you call it, it's vitally necessary for every Christian!

A consistent time in the Word of God will change the way that we think about this world, our own personal priorities (Romans 12:1,2), and we'll begin to see things the way Jesus sees them. By having a daily time in the Word of God, Jesus will set us free from bad ideas and toxic sins in our lives (John 8:31,32), and He'll be blessed by meeting us in a time of intimate worship and communion as well! (Luke 10:38-42)

For your devotional time in the Word, start by praying to the Lord, and asking Him to lead you to a specific book of the New Testament. One of the four Gospels is always a great choice, especially the Gospel of John. Take a book of the New Testament, and read it in small sections, on a consistent daily basis. These small sections of Scripture are usually separated with subtitles in your Bible, and are divided that way on purpose by the translators. Remember, *quality* is much more important than *quantity* in your Bible reading, so I'd recommend reading and deeply meditating on one or two of these small sections every day. This will benefit you much more than reading two or three chapters every day, as that's far too much information to remember, or work through in daily meditation. *Quality* is far more important than *quantity!*

Practically speaking, I'd recommend at least 15 to 30 minutes of Bible reading. Every day, **read** the next section of verses in that book, **think** about what they mean, **meditate** on them, and **write down** how they can be applied to your life that week. Read that book, in small sections, chapter by chapter and verse by verse (Isaiah 28:10,13) until you've finished it completely. This will take time, but remember, it's about *quality* not *quantity!* Go through the books of the Bible slowly, one at a time, and you'll grow at an incredible rate spiritually! (Read 2 Timothy 3:16)

If necessary, set your alarm clock to get up 30 minutes earlier, to give you ample time to sit at the feet of Jesus, and hear His Words for *your* life. (Luke 10:38-42) Do this consistently for about 3 weeks, and it will become a natural habit. This is a very important use of our time, and it must *always* remain a top priority in our daily schedules. (Read Psalm 1; Psalm 138:2; Joshua 1:8-9; John 8:31,32; Acts 2:42)

#2 – Spend Time Serving Jesus

Another investment of your time towards Heaven, should be to serve Christ in your local church. One of the best ways a Christian can use their time, is to get consistently involved in serving in a weekly ministry in their local church fellowship.

Jesus told us that one of the "marks of greatness" in His Kingdom was that of serving others (Matt 20:25-28), as He so perfectly demonstrated for us during His life, ministry, teachings, and death. In the Kingdom, it's obvious who is mature spiritually, as their lives are primarily about *giving* and not about *getting*. This is an obvious sign of growth in the life of a believer, when the focus shifts from *being served* to *serving others* when they come to church!

There are many aspects of the Christian life that you simply won't be able to experience at a deeper level, until you get involved in your local church and begin to serve others. Biblical concepts such as humility, sacrifice, love, forgiveness, faithfulness and a host of others, are truly learned when you enter the arena of Christian service!

I encourage you to pray and ask God to show you where to get involved in your local church family, with the unique gifts and talents that He's given to you. Say *"Lord, how can I serve you?"* and He is faithful to answer that prayer!

Even if it's just once a month in your church's Nursery, Children's Ministry, Ushering, or Greeting, it'll be a wonderful opportunity for you to grow spiritually, and to make great investments into the Kingdom of Heaven. If you're *not serving* at all in your church, use your time to serve at least a little bit and (trust me) your pastors and leaders will be very thankful that the Lord brought you their way!

If you're *already serving* in your local church, I challenge you, serve just a little bit more. Prayerfully increase your Heavenly investment to a greater degree, in your local church family. For example, if you're serving once a month, then try twice a month. If you're serving twice a month, try to serve three times a month. Just pray and let the Lord lead you in your service. Invest just a little more of your time to for Christ, beyond whatever level you're currently at. It'll be a blessing for you, a big help to your local ministry, and a huge investment for you in the Kingdom of Heaven! (Read Hebrews 6:10; Matthew 25:21)

#3 – Spend Time In Prayer & Worship

A third way to use the precious resource of your time, is to spend it doing what you were created for: *worshipping your Creator!* When a Christian intentionally dedicates large portions of time to seeking the Lord through prayer and worship, it's one of the best uses of their time imaginable!

As you habitually get up in the morning and spend time in the Scriptures, *this* is the ideal time to spend in prayer and communion with Jesus. When you begin your devotions, I encourage you to start with at least 5 minutes of prayer. This is the perfect opportunity to speak to the Lord, confess any sin that's keeping you from Him (1 John 1:9), express your heart of thanksgiving for all that He's done for you lately (Luke 17:11-19), or simply intercede for a loved one before the Lord in prayer.

Also, when you finish your time with the Lord, it's a great idea to close it off with prayer again. This is an ideal moment to reflect on and thank God for all the great things He showed you that morning in His Word. Through a time of simple prayer, you can reflect upon all the things that the Lord revealed to you during your devotions. Starting and ending your *"Devo Time"* in prayer, is a great way to grow in Christ!

However, worshipping the Lord in song is also a great joy, as you seek the Lord in private. I encourage you to sing a song or two worship to the Lord every morning, as you sit before Him. If you're not a musical person, simply play a worship song from your phone, tablet, or computer and sing along with it. This will develop within you a heart of sitting before Jesus, in simple praise and surrender, bowing your heart before Him!

Be sure to open you heart during this time of worship, lift your hands in surrender, and close your eyes to be undistracted and focused on the Lord. Ask the Lord to fill you with His Holy Spirit during this time (Acts 1:8) so you can have power over your flesh during your workday (Romans 8:13; Galatians 5:13). Cultivating a lifestyle of worship will revolutionize your life as a disciple of Christ!

#4 – Spend Time Fellowshipping With Christians

Finally, another great use of your time is to fellowship with other believers. The word for *"fellowship"* in the New Testament is the word *"koinonia"*, which is a very rich and colorful word in the Greek language. There really isn't a direct translation, but it can mean *"sharing life together, joint participation, oneness, communion together"*.

This is what the Lord desires for His children: sharing their lives with one another, spending rich time together, and growing in relationships with each other!

As we look at the Early Church in the Book of Acts, this is exactly what they did. We read that they spent their time fellowshipping with each other, sharing their food, and serving one another (Acts 2:42-47). This shows us that as a Christian, it's important for you to consistently spend time with the other "citizens of Heaven" (Phil 3:20) and grow in relationship with other believers!

One of the best ways to do this, is *consistently* attending your local church throughout the week. Being an active member in your church family is vital to keep growing as a Christian, and investing your time towards Heavenly goals. The local church is a kind of "Heavenly Embassy" that Jesus has planted all over the earth, to conduct "spiritual operations" for His Kingdom. To be separated from your local church, and not be a regular part of it, is to separate yourself from the major instrument that the Lord is using on earth to accomplish the work of Heaven!

The writer of Hebrews warned us against the danger of not fellowshipping with other believers (Heb 10:25). Paul told us that all Christians are a part of the Body of Christ globally, and a local body of believers as well. (1 Cor 12; Col 2:19)

Since this is so clearly taught in scripture, a great use of your time then is to attend multiple weekly services at your church, become involved in serving in a weekly ministry, and joining a small Home Group that fits your situation in life. During these times of fellowship, be intentional and seek to cultivate friendships with others believers. Go out to lunch with people, get to know them, spend time together, sharing what the Lord has done in your lives. Growing in fellowship and sharing life with other Christians in and out of church is a great investment of your time towards Heaven!

Time is a precious but perishable resource that the Lord has given you. If you spend it wisely, by studying the Scriptures, serving in ministry, growing in prayer and worship, and deepening your Christian fellowship, you'll be using your time wisely... and as a *great* investment in the Kingdom of Heaven!

Heavenly Investment #2:

My Treasure!

Another powerful tool that God has given you for the expansion of His Kingdom, are your financial resources. We've all been given a certain amount of money from the Lord, and the highest use of those resources is to do exactly what Jesus taught us in Matthew's Gospel:

"..lay up for yourselves treasures in Heaven, where neither moth nor rust destroys and where thieves do not break in and steal."
– Matthew 6:20 NKJV

By investing your financial resources and "treasures" into your local church, ministries, and Christian outreaches, you are actually investing it into the Kingdom of God, and being obedient to the command of Christ! The major principle to grasp in this area of discipleship is simple:

Everything you own is God's... absolutely <u>everything!</u>

We often refer to our possessions as *"my money, my resources, my property"* but in actuality, everything that is under your control, really belongs to Christ. We are simply ***"stewards"*** of all the financial resources in our care. A ***"steward"*** is an old English word, for a servant who is put in charge of a wealthy person's assets, employed for the sole purpose of managing them wisely, according to the wishes of the owner. The money under his control, isn't his money, but the steward distributes and spends it in a way that accomplishes the desires of his master.

This is the biblical idea of Christians and their finances – we are simply managers and stewards of Jesus' resources. Everything we own, is put into our hands by the Lord, and we are simply called to properly employ it for His Kingdom and His eternal purposes! The obvious question then, is this:

How are <u>you</u> using the Lord's money?

If your finances and your money were represented by another three-dimensional pie graph, how big would the different slices be? How much money are you currently spending on the different areas of your life? How much of your money do you pay towards your rent or your mortgage? How much do you spend on your water and electric? How much do you give to the IRS? As unpleasant as it may be, it's important to give to Caesar what is Caesar's, like Jesus taught us to. (Read Matthew 22:21)

How much money do you spend on entertainment? How much money do you spend on vacation? How much money do you spend on miscellaneous things? Though you may not have much money, that's not really the issue. Remember, at the Judgement Seat of Christ, we're *all* going to be held accountable for how we used our finances in this life, whether we had a lot or a little. We're *all* going to stand before Jesus and He's going to ask us, *"I only gave you a certain amount of money, but how did you use it? How did you manage the resources I gave you to expand My Kingdom?"*

Here are 4 simple strategies to use your financial resources for the Kingdom of God, and do as Christ commanded us–store up treasures in Heaven:

#1 – Worship The Lord With Your Tithe

Though it's a sensitive topic to some, biblically we must ask ourselves these questions:

Do I tithe regularly?
Do I give consistently of my income to the Lord?
Is my worship to Christ reflected in my financial giving?

Contrary to what many believe, in the Old Testament, the Jews did not just "tithe" by giving 10% of their income to the Lord. They were commanded to give about 28% of their total yearly income, as an expression of worship. Altogether, for the temple fees, taxes, tithe offerings–the Jews gave approximately 28% of their finances to the Lord, in obedience and adoration. However, as Christians, we are never commanded to give a specific amount of our income to the Lord. Paul simply tells us in 2 Corinthians 8-9 that we're to be cheerful, prayerful, and worshipful in our financial worship.

Nonetheless, it's interesting that 400 years before Moses and the Jewish Law, there lived a famous biblical patriarch, named Abraham. In **Genesis 18** Abraham met a man named Melchizedek, a mysterious Priest of the Most High God. Can you guess how Abraham worshipped the Lord in front of Melchizedek? He gave Melchizedek 10% of all of his possessions! He tithed to Melchizedek who was at the very least, a priest of God, and very possibly Christ Himself, as the writer of the book of Hebrews seems to indicate. (Read Hebrews 5:6,10; 6:20; 7:1-9)

Isn't it interesting that Abraham tithed before the Law even existed? Abraham is held up in the New Testament, as a great example of faith, an example of obedience for Christians. And in this area of financial worship, I think he's a great example for us as well. Unfortunately, as many studies across America indicate, the average Christian only gives about 2.5% of their income, about $5 to $10 a week, in financial worship at their local church. One has to wonder, if a central element of worship is sacrifice, does *this* even qualify as adoration in the eyes of the Lord? (Read 2 Samuel 24:19-25)

This is a tragic reality, as the Lord wants to do so many things *in* and *thru* the local church. A powerful tool that God currently uses in the world, to expand His Kingdom and spread the Gospel, is money. The Lord uses money as a tool to get Christian radio programs going, buy bibles, feed and clothe the homeless, pay the rent for church buildings, pro-vide salaries to Christian staff workers, along with a thousand other activities that expand the Kingdom of Heaven on earth. Financial resources are a pow-erful tool the Lord has placed in our care, to spread the Gospel and to bring people into His Kingdom!

I challenge you, begin to worship the Lord con-sistently thru your giving, if you don't do so already. Only give to the Lord if it's from a heart of love and true worship, but I encourage you to begin to use the finances God has given you in this biblical way. In doing so, you'll be investing significantly in the Kingdom of Heaven!

#2-Use Your Money to Help the Needy

Another great way that you can invest your financial resources for the work of Heaven, is to help those around you in need. One of the major reasons that the Lord has prospered you financially, is so that you can come to the aid of those in your sphere of life, that need financial help. Using your money in this way is one of the best expressions of "pure religion" according to the Scriptures:

> *"Pure and undefiled religion before*
> *God and the Father is this:*
> *to visit orphans and widows in their trouble,*
> *and to keep oneself unspotted from the world."*
> *- James 1:27 NKJV*

If you personally know anyone that is a widow, orphan, or simply in a dire situation where they could use financial assistance, it's one of the best investments of your money for God's Kingdom. In the eyes of the Lord, this is a pure display of a heart that truly loves Him!

This model of using financial resources to help those in need, was first practiced by the Early Church. The first 30 years of Early Church history are recorded in the Book of Acts, and it's obvious that they also used their finances to help each other, as followers of Christ:

"And they continued steadfastly in the apostles' doctrine and fellowship, in the breaking of bread, and in prayers. Then fear came upon every soul, and many wonders and signs were done through the apostles. Now all who believed were together, and had all things in common, and sold their possessions and goods, and divided them among all, as anyone had need. So continuing daily with one accord in the temple, and breaking bread from house to house, they ate their food with gladness and simplicity of heart, praising God and having favor with all the people. And the Lord added to the church daily those who were being saved."
- Acts 2:42-47 NKJV

Our Christian practices and behaviors need to be based on the Scriptures and this practice of financial benevolence has a strong biblical foundation. Something the Early Church was deeply engaged in was the selling of their possessions and sharing their goods and food with those in need. To live in this generous way not only reflects the heart of Christ, but also makes a great investment in the Kingdom of Heaven!

Paul the Apostle, knowing this to be true, was engaged from time to time, in gathering financial gifts from certain churches, to send them to very poor congregations that were struggling financially. Historically, we know that the church in Jerusalem went "bankrupt" and was existing in abject poverty for some time. Though we don't know the specific cause, we do know that Paul urged the Christians in other churches to rally to their aid, and assist them financially. He wrote this to the church in Corinth:

"Now concerning the collection for the saints, as I have given orders to the churches of Galatia, so you must do also: On the first day of the week let each one of you lay something aside, storing up as he may prosper, that there be no collections when I come. And when I come, whomever you approve by your letters I will send to bear your gift to Jerusalem."
- 1 Corinthians 16:1-4 NKJV

As you can clearly see, Paul clearly taught the practice of using our financial resources to help any hurting brothers or sisters around us in financial need. It's also good to keep in mind that, while the Lord loves all men and wants us to do the same, according to the Scriptures, helping a Christian financially should always take precedence over aiding those who are unbelievers. Paul declared this to the Christians of Galatia:

"Therefore, as we have opportunity, let us do
good to all, especially to those who
are of the household of faith."
- Galatians 6:10 NKJV

If the choice must be made, seek to first help the believer and follower of Christ, as they are your brother or sister, and a child of your King!

So, do *you* know a Christian single mother that might need some mechanical repairs on her car, but can't afford it? Do *you* know a teenager that needs a financial sponsorship to attend the Youth Retreat and hear the Gospel? Are *you* aware of a poor family in your church that is behind on their bills? These are simple but powerful ways to show the love of Christ, and expand His Kingdom upon the earth!

#3–Use Your Finances to Support Christian Ministries

Another way I encourage you to use the money the Lord has entrusted you with, is to prayerfully direct it toward Christian ministries that are effective and diligent in preaching the Gospel, and spreading the Word of God throughout the world. One of the best investments that you can make into the Kingdom, is to find a ministry that is doing exactly what Jesus commanded in the Sermon on the Mount:

"But seek first the kingdom of God and His
righteousness, and all these things shall be
added to you."
- Matthew 6:33 NKJV

Jesus clearly challenged His disciples to make the expansion of His Kingdom the *first* priority of their lives. Along with living a holy life of worship, seeking to spread Christ's Kingdom into the hearts and lives of those around us, should be our #1 *top priority* in this life!

The word Jesus used for *"seek"* is the Greek word *"zētéō"* meaning *"to seek after, to strive after, or to strongly crave something." That* is how the Lord wants us to feel about expanding His Kingdom! It should be something that we *strongly crave* to do, and our *highest priority* in this life!

One of the most effective ways we can accomplish this is to funnel our financial resources to specific ministries and churches that are effectively teaching God's Word, discipling others, and reaching their communities with the Gospel! Whenever you financially partner with such ministries, you are helping them accomplish their mission of expanding Christ's Kingdom here on earth. It's one of the greatest investments you can make with your money for the cause of Heaven!

Jesus went on to caution us that we shouldn't be primarily investing in the things of this earth, but rather fixated on the things of the Kingdom. He put it like this:

"Do not lay up for yourselves treasures on earth, where moth and rust destroy and where thieves break in and steal; but lay up for yourselves treasures in heaven, where neither moth nor rust destroys and where thieves do not break in and steal. For where your treasure is, there your

heart will be also."
- Matthew 6:19-21 NKJV

Either we're storing up treasures on earth, or we're "sending them ahead" by investing them in works and outreaches for Christ. Obviously, the ones that will yield eternal dividends, are those that fund and support the expansion of God's Kingdom.

Even in the days of Jesus, many people recognized the reality of this principle. Many of the women that followed in Christ's entourage during His earthly ministry, were wealthy ladies who used their finances to support the practical needs of Jesus and His team of disciples. We're told a few of their names in the Gospel of Luke where we read this:

".. Joanna the wife of Chuza, Herod's steward, and Susanna, and many others who provided for Him from their substance."
- Luke 8:3 NKJV

Apparently, these women were wives of wealthy individuals, and decided that a good use of their money was to support the earthly ministry of Christ. These ladies enabled Jesus' ministry team to physically have what they needed to preach the Gospel, help those around them, and expand the Kingdom. Imagine the reward that these faithful sisters will enjoy in Heaven! They financially supported Jesus and His disciples for about 3 years, enabling them to change the lives and eternal destinies of countless people in the ages to come. What an incredible reward they'll receive from their Lord and Master, when He rules over the earth, in the Kingdom of Heaven!

However, *you* have that same opportunity in your life, as you partner with biblical ministries and churches, that are aggressively expanding the Kingdom of Jesus in our time! This is a very effective and practical way for you to *"store up treasures in Heaven"* as Christ commanded us!

Heavenly Investment #3:

My Talents!

A third and very important Kingdom investment for every disciple of Christ, is that of Spiritual Gifts and Talents. These are some of the greatest resources the Lord has committed into your care. Learning to use them diligently and effectively for Christ, is one of the greatest things you can do for the Kingdom. There are 3 things you must do to effectively invest your Spiritual Gifts and Talents for Heaven:

#1–DISCOVER your Talents for Christ's Kingdom

The first thing to do is *discover* and learn what the gifts and talents are that Christ has given you. Before you can learn how to be effective with the abilities Christ has put inside you, they must first be identified.

However, let me make a distinction between natural talents and spiritual gifts: Talents are natural skills that you possess (i.e. musical skill, mathematics, languages, practical skills, athletic ability, photographic memory, etc..) that can be used in service to the Lord in different areas of life. However, since they are *natural*, even non-Christians can have these talents, and many times are just as good at using them (or even better) than Christians are!

Spiritual Gifts, on the other hand, are *supernatural* and given to you through God, the Holy Spirit. These belong only to Christians, and are dispersed among believers in hopes that we'll use them for the glory of Christ and the expansion of His Kingdom! Paul writes much about the Spiritual Gifts, and how they're supposed to operate in the life of a believer. He taught this to the Christians in Corinth:

"There are diversities of gifts, but the same Spirit. There are differences of ministries, but the same Lord. And there are diversities of activities, but it is the same God who works all in all. But the manifestation of the Spirit is given to each one for the profit of all.."
- 1 Corinthians 12:4-7 NKJV

Here, we can learn many things, but Paul is very clear about one important truth: every believer in Christ has *at least* one spiritual gift. He says that *"the manifestation of the Spirit is given to each one for the profit of all.."* Every disciple of Jesus possesses at least one such gift from the Holy Spirit. But the central question for each of us is this:

"Do you know what *your* Spiritual Gifts and Talents are?"

Unfortunately, many Christians would have to answer that they don't know. From my own experience as a pastor, it's sad to say that a large number of believers have no idea of the spiritual gifts deposited inside of them by the Lord.

Here, from chapters 12 thru 14, Paul is describing to the Corinthians a category of spiritual gifts that we could call the *"Manifestational Gifts."* As you might guess, these gifts "manifest" the presence and power of the Holy Spirit during particular times. These are gifts that a believer can operate in, at different instances, depending on how the Spirit chooses to use them. Regardless of your understanding (or lack thereof) of these Spiritual Gifts, you possess at least one, according to the Scriptures.

In Ephesians, Paul describes yet another category of Spiritual Gifts that we call the *"Ministry Gifts."* This is a fitting title, for all of them describe different ministry offices that exist within the church. In chapter four of Ephesians Paul describes them like this:

"And He Himself gave some to be apostles, some prophets, some evangelists, and some pastors and teachers, for the equipping of the saints for the work of ministry, for the edifying of the body of Christ.."
- Ephesians 4:11-12 NKJV

You yourself may be called by the Lord to function in one of these ministry "offices" in your local church. It may be for a time in the future, when you've been trained and prepared, but nonetheless the Lord may have called you to it. Notice how Paul says these individuals themselves are *"gifts"* to the local church, given by Christ to the congregations. If you have faithful ministers, pastors, or teachers in your local church, you should love them, honor them, and thank God for them–they are His *gifts* to your church family!

A third and final category of Spiritual Gifts that Paul mentions is in Romans 12. We call these the *"Motivational Gifts"* for they describe a spiritual motivation that the Lord puts inside of you as a Christian. It's like a spiritual "programming" or "operating system" that the Lord engineered inside of you. In one way or another, it's why you act the way you do, and have the perspective you do as a Christian. Paul put it like this:

"For as we have many members in one body, but all the members do not have the same function, so we, being many, are one body in Christ, and individually members of one another. Having then gifts differing according to the grace that is given to us, let us use them: if prophecy, let us prophesy in proportion to our faith; or ministry, let us use it in our ministering; he who teaches, in teaching; he who exhorts, in exhortation; he who gives, with liberality; he who leads, with diligence; he who shows mercy, with cheerfulness."
- Romans 12:4-8 NKJV

In my opinion as a pastor, these are by far the most important spiritual gifts in the life of any Christian. The reason for this, is that you operate in these "Motivational Gifts" every day of your life! They are a large part of *why* you are, the *way* you are. The reason why a certain person considers details, information, and shades of meaning important is because they possess the Motivational Gift of "Teaching." The explanation for why a person feels a supernatural desire to reach out to those in need, and empathizes in a very sensitive way with people's pain, is because they have the Motivational Gift of "Mercy." And so on, with all of the Motivational Gifts mentioned by Paul in Romans 12.

Regardless of the category *("Manifestational", "Ministry", or "Motivational")*, your Spiritual Gifts need to be discovered to help you fully become the person that Christ has called you to be for His Kingdom. The best way to do this, is speak with your local church pastors and teachers, and they'll be able to help you understand how the Lord has equipped *you* in this area of Spiritual Gifts. From their experience, understanding of the Scriptures, and even particular "tests" they may have developed, these ministers will be able to help you *discover* the Spiritual Gifts that the Lord has put inside of you to be effective as His servant, and to expand His Heavenly Kingdom!

#2–DEVELOP your Talents for Christ's Kingdom

Once you discover your Spiritual Gifts, and have a better idea of how the Lord has equipped you, the next step is to *develop* those abilities for the glory of God. Once you understand what abilities the Lord has given you to serve Him, it's up to you to *develop* and mature those Gifts to grow into their fullness and maturity, to serve Jesus effectively!

We all have to start somewhere, and this means that it will take you time to develop your Spiritual Gifts. A season of preparation is always necessary, as every believer's Spiritual Gifts begin in small ways. In speaking of small beginnings, the prophet Zechariah had this to say:

"For who has despised the day of small things?"
- Zechariah 4:10 NKJV

This is recorded in the Word of God, because it's natural for us to despise small beginnings, or look down on the time when our Spiritual Gifts are still immature and not fully developed. But when you find yourself in this stage of growth, know that it's completely normal, and very necessary. As a matter of fact, even the great King David had a prolonged period of preparation in his own life to help him become the king that he was called to be. In 1 Samuel 17, we read the words of David to king Saul:

"Then David said to Saul, "Let no man's heart fail because of him; your servant will go and fight with this Philistine." And Saul said to David, "You are not able to go against this Philistine to fight with him; for you are a youth, and he a man of war from his youth." David said to Saul, "Your servant used to keep his father's sheep, and when a lion or a bear came and took a lamb out of the flock, I went out after it and struck it, and delivered the lamb from its mouth; and when it arose against me, I caught it by its beard, and struck and killed it. Your servant has killed both

lion and bear; and this uncircumcised Philistine will be like one of them, seeing he has defied the armies of the living God." Moreover David said, "The Lord, who delivered me from the paw of the lion and from the paw of the bear, He will deliver me from the hand of this Philistine."
- 1 Samuel 17:32-37 NKJV

It's obvious that the Lord had been preparing David in secret, long before He ever set him upon the throne. Even as a teenager, probably 15 years of age, David entered into hand-to-hand combat with a lion! On a separate occasion, he fought a bear with his bare hands–amazing! However, it was on this day, as he stood before Saul, that David perceived that the lion had *prepared* him for the bear; and the bear *prepared* him for the giant; and the giant would further *prepare* him for his calling as king of Israel! It was all preparation for what lay in store for David next. And so it is with you and I, along with every other great man or woman of God in Scripture. Preparation is a vital component in our spiritual growth as well!

Didn't Joshua have to be *prepared* by being a servant and soldier...before becoming a general? Wasn't Moses *prepared* for 40 years in Midian as a shepherd and servant...before becoming a deliverer? Didn't Timothy have to be *prepared* as a follower and student of Paul's...before he pastored the church at Ephesus? Wasn't Abraham *prepared* through 10 test of developing faith...before he could become the "Father of Faith?" Didn't even Paul have to be *prepared* for years in the desert and his hometown of Cilicia...before becoming the Apostle to the Gentiles?

Just like a good soldier, a strong athlete, or a dependable building...preparation is a key ingredient to success. Before there can be a *public victory*, there must first be *preparation privately!* After your Spiritual Gift is discovered, it needs to be developed by using it in small ways, in order to grow in your confidence, and the effectiveness of your gift. Start using your Gift whenever you can, and you will see it develop and grow stronger and stronger over time!

#3–DEPLOY your Talents for Christ's Kingdom

After your spiritual gifts have been discovered and more fully developed, then comes the time to fully *deploy* them for Christ. By this, I mean that over time, the Lord will open to you significant and meaningful opportunities, to use your Spiritual Gifts like never before. You need to seize these opportunities, unleash your Gifts for Christ, thereby making a significant investment in the Kingdom of Heaven!

Though you may have served the Lord before, there will probably come the chance to step into a new *direction* of ministry, or a new *kind* of ministry, using the particular gifts He's given you. More than likely, this "open door" for ministry, will have something to do with the Lord's ultimate calling on your life. Stepping up in faith to serve the Lord is how you will become the man or woman of God, that you were always called to be! (Read Ephesians 2:10) This very thing happened to Isaiah in the Old Testament, and he described it like this:

"Also I heard the voice of the Lord, saying:
"Whom shall I send, who will go for Us?"

I said, "Here am I! Send me."
- Isaiah 6:8 NKJV

Isaiah overheard a conversation within the Godhead of the Father, Son, and Spirit. In that moment, as the Trinity was seeking a person go on their behalf and spread their message, Isaiah simple said *"Yes! Send me!"* He saw the Lord opening up an opportunity, and he *took* it! He *seized* the day for the Lord...by *deploying* his Gift. He knew it was a door of opportunity the Lord opened to him, and so he walked thru it!

The same thing will happen in your life as well. The Lord will present *you* with specific opportunities to use and deploy your gift for His Kingdom. It's in these moments that you will have to intentionally decide to use your gift to serve Christ and expand His Kingdom. This is when a Christian really begins to mature, as they intentionally practice the continual use of their gifts, in every situation the Lord puts in front of them, for His glory and for their growth!

Paul exhorts us to develop a type of lifestyle in which we are always seeking to deploy our gifts and be active in service to the Lord. He puts it like this in his letter to the Corinthians:

"Therefore, my beloved brethren, be steadfast, immovable, always abounding in the work of the Lord, knowing that your labor is not in vain in the Lord."
- 1 Corinthians 15:58 NKJV

Paul tells us that the deploying and utilizing of our gifts is never in vain, especially in light of the promises of Heaven and the Resurrection body. Every single act of service that a Christian performs for Jesus and His Kingdom, takes on significant meaning and carries with it an eternal impact! Jesus taught us that no act of service for His Kingdom, no matter how small, would ever be forgotten or overlooked by Him.

"He who receives a prophet in the name of a prophet shall receive a prophet's reward. And he who receives a righteous man in the name of a righteous man shall receive a righteous man's reward. And whoever gives one of these little ones only a cup of cold water in the name of a disciple, assuredly, I say to you, he shall by no means lose his reward."
- Matthew 10:41-42 NKJV

Amazing! Every single instance of deploying your Spiritual Gifts for the sake of Heaven will be rewarded by Jesus in the Kingdom. What a strong motivation this should be for us to habitually deploy our Spiritual Gifts and natural talents in serving our local churches!

Jesus would go on to say that one of the marks of serious disciples is that they would be aggressive in the deployment of their Spiritual Gifts for the sake of His Kingdom. He put it like this:

"And from the days of John the Baptist until now the kingdom of heaven suffers violence,

and the violent take it by force."
- Matthew 11:12 NKJV

In this famous play on words, Jesus taught us that though the Kingdom has been violently and aggressively opposed by satan and his forces, faithful disciples should be equally aggressive (in a spiritual sense) of discovering, developing, and deploying their gifts for Christ and the cause of Heaven. Living like this is one of the best ways to ensure that you're making continual investments into the Lord's everlasting Kingdom!

Heavenly Investment #4:

My Tools!

Finally, after examining how we can live for Heaven by investing our Time, Treasure, and Talents, there's still one area of resources that we can employ in seeking to live for God's Kingdom. There are special and specific "Tools" that the Lord has given every Christian to expand and broaden the influence of His Kingdom. Regardless of you how much time you have, or the kind of Spiritual Gifts you possess, these "Tools" are available to every disciple that wants to use them. They are the "Tools" of the Gospel, the power of Prayer, the eternal Word of God, and your personal Testimony! Let's examine each of them, as we bring our study of Heaven to a close.

#1–Use the Tool of the GOSPEL for Christ's Kingdom

One of the most powerful spiritual tools that you possess to expand the Kingdom, is the Gospel. This is what we commonly call the "Good News" and is the central message of the New Testament, about Who Jesus Christ truly is, and how He will graciously save anyone who comes to Him in simple faith.

Of course, before we speak of using the Gospel, we need to first define what it is. It may surprise you to hear that a great many Christians are confused about what the core elements of the Gospel really are. Though it's not very complicated, it is very important to understand this, so that we can be confident we're sharing the right information with unbelievers about how Christ can save them.

Essentially, there are three core elements to the Gospel. If we read 1 Corinthians 15:1-4 and cross reference it with Romans 10, there are three main truths to the Good News of the New Testament:

1. **Jesus is God the Son**, who came into the world as a true human being.
2. **Jesus died for the sins of the world**, as a substitutionary sacrifice.
3. **Jesus physically rose from the grave**, proving his Deity.

When we share with people around us, if any of these 3 elements is missing, then we're not really telling them the New Testament Gospel. It's vital that we help people understand that **Jesus is God**, and not merely a teacher, prophet, or holy man. Next, we let them know that the reason Christ came to earth is to **die for the sins of the world**, thereby making a way for us to be saved from the eternal punishment we deserve. Lastly, we share that we know Christ is God and that His sacrifice was accepted, because **He rose physically from the grave**, just as He said He would.

It's by believing the truth of these 3 biblical facts, and asking Christ to apply it their own heart, that a person can be forgiven of all sins past, present, and future. It's by surrendering to Jesus as Lord and Savior, on the basis of these 3 great truths, that a person is saved from eternal judgment. This is the New Testament Gospel and the "Good News" of salvation!

As we said, sharing *this* Gospel with those around you is one of the best ways to serve the Lord, and to invest in the Kingdom of Heaven. Paul told us why he was so compelled to share the Good News in his lifetime:

> *"For I am not ashamed of the gospel of Christ, for it is the power of God to salvation for everyone who believes, for the Jew first and also for the Greek."*
> *- Romans 1:16 NKJV*

He tells us that the Gospel is the *"power of God"* to save people. This is the Greek word *"dynamis"* from which we get the words *"dynamic"* or even *"dynamite."* He is telling us that the Gospel of Jesus Christ has explosive power to transform and rescue those around us...*if we'll just share it with them!*

Maybe this is why believers are sometimes *"ashamed"* or timid to share the Gospel with our friends and family. Could it be that we don't truly believe in the dynamic spiritual power of the Gospel to save? However, all we need to do is simply remember how it transformed *our* lives when we first came to Christ, and it will be clear to us that the Gospel is what our unsaved friends and family really need! Sharing this Good News of salvation found in Christ alone is one of the most urgent needs in our world today. Jesus told us that this was one of the central missions for His disciples, just before He ascended to Heaven:

"And Jesus came and spoke to them, saying, "All authority has been given to Me in heaven and on earth. Go therefore and make disciples of all the nations, baptizing them in the name of the Father and of the Son and of the Holy Spirit, teaching them to observe all things that I have commanded you; and lo, I am with you always, even to the end of the age." Matthew 28:18-20 NKJV

A man's last words are extremely important, and with Christ this is definitely the case. As He was leaving the disciples, and ascending to Heaven, Jesus commissioned and commanded them to go into all the world and share His truth with the unbelieving gentile nations. He assured them that His power and authority would guard and guide them, as they spread the Gospel throughout the entire known world of their day!

In the book of Acts, Luke tells us an additional statement that Jesus uttered, just before He ascended. He recorded these words:

"But you shall receive power when the Holy Spirit has come upon you; and you shall be witnesses to Me in Jerusalem, and in all Judea and Samaria, and to the end of the earth."
– Acts 1:8 NKJV

Here again we see that Jesus was supremely concerned with the disciples sharing the Gospel. As they spread throughout the their world, they were to bear witness of the fact that Christ is the God-Man, that He died for the sins of the world, and physically rose from the dead, opening up the way of salvation for all of mankind! Sharing and preaching the Good News was the mission statement of the Early Church, and the "battle plan" of God to expand Christ's Kingdom upon the earth...and it still is today!

Paul the apostle would even go so far as to tell us, that it was in the express will of God, that every person on earth know the truth about Jesus Christ. He wrote these words:

"..God our Savior, who desires all men to be saved and to come to the knowledge of the truth. For there is one God and one Mediator between God and men, the Man Christ Jesus.."
1 Timothy 2:3-5 NKJV

Though we may not know the will of God in all areas of life, there are many issues that are detailed for us in the Word. This is one of them: He desires for *every* person on earth to come to a saving knowledge of Jesus Christ, and understand the truth of *Who* He is and *what* He has done for us, thru His cross and resurrection! Knowing this, it should give us great motivation and inspiration in using the tool of the Gospel, in expanding the Kingdom of Heaven on earth, and bringing those around us to a saving knowledge of Christ!

#2–Use the Tool of PRAYER for Christ's Kingdom

Another great tool we have at our disposal, as we live for Heaven and invest in eternity, is the mighty weapon of prayer! This is one of the single greatest powers that the Lord has made available to us as believers–to unleash the might and strength of God into our daily situations, simply by asking!

In the book of Ephesians, as he's discussing spiritual warfare and the "Armor of God", Paul ends the section by mentioning the weapon of prayer, when he writes:

"..praying always with all prayer and supplication in the Spirit, being watchful to this end with all perseverance and supplication for all the saints—and for me, that utterance may be given to me, that I may open my mouth boldly to make known the mystery of the gospel.."
Ephesians 6:18-19 NKJV

Unbeknownst to many Christians, prayer is listed in this section on spiritual warfare as one of our only offensive weapons as believers. Just as soldiers can use their satellite radios to call in air support and air strikes upon their enemies, prayer allows us to call in the "big guns" for spiritual warfare and pushing back the kingdom of darkness! Prayer gives the us the ability to invite the infinite God to unleash His power and influence into a situation, making it a vital and necessary tool in the spiritual "arsenal" of every disciple!

Paul also told us the extent of what the Lord could do for us, if we'll just come to Him and ask for His help. He described God's ability to help us like this:

"Now to Him who is able to do exceedingly abundantly above all that we ask or think, according to the power that works in us.."
Ephesians 3:20 NKJV

Did you notice the superlative words that Paul used in this verse? He said that God is able to do *"exceedingly"* and *"abundantly"* and *"above all"* that is even conceivable to our thoughts or requests to Him! If we truly believed that, how much more would we use the tool of prayer in expanding God's Kingdom?

Jesus went on to remind us that though something might be impossible for humans, it is not so with the Lord God:

"Jesus looked at them and said,
'With men it is impossible, but not with God;
for with God all things are possible.'"
- Mark 10:27 NKJV

Many times it's through the powerful and mighty weapon of prayer that the seemingly impossible is achieved. Through a praying believer, Christ can work miracles and wonders that are far beyond human ability. If we would only believe this, it would motivate us to keep pressing on in prayer, until we see the Lord moving and working in our situation! To this end, Jesus gave us a wonderful encouragement to never stop or faint in our praying, when He taught us:

"Ask, and it will be given to you; seek, and you will find; knock, and it will be opened to you. For everyone who asks receives, and he who seeks finds, and to him who knocks it will be opened."
Matthew 7:7-8 NKJV

These original words in the Greek language imply a continual action that never stops. It literally means to *"ask and keep on asking"*, to *"seek and keep on seeking"*, and to *"knock and keep on knocking"* in prayer. How wonderful it would be if we truly did this in our prayer lives! How much we would see the Lord work if we truly believed and practiced what the Lord taught us about prayer!

In seeking to live for the Kingdom of Heaven, the tool of prayer is surely one of the most powerful and effective in the arsenal of any Christian. May we use it more consistently as we labor for eternity!

#3–Use the Tool of GOD'S WORD for Christ's Kingdom

Another weapon that we've been given as believers, to wage war on the kingdom of darkness, and expand the Kingdom of Heaven, is the Word of God. As a Bible teaching pastor, I see this as one of the most vital tools in the life of every New Testament church and individual believer today!

In describing God's Word and how it comes into play in spiritual warfare, Paul wrote these famous and well known words to the Ephesians:

"Stand therefore, having girded your waist with truth, having put on the breastplate of righteousness, and having shod your feet with the preparation of the gospel of peace; above all, taking the shield of faith with which you will be able to quench all the fiery darts of the wicked one. And take the helmet of salvation, and the sword of the Spirit, which is the word of God.."
Ephesians 6:14-18 NKJV

Paul tells us that the Word of God is comparable to a sword used in personal hand-to-hand combat by a Roman soldier. It's interesting to note that the original Greek word used here, speaks of a short sword or long dagger, meaning it was a fight that was up close and personal. The Scriptures are the *"Sword of the Spirit"* and one of the greatest offensive weapons we possess in our struggle against the kingdom of darkness. The writer to the Hebrews described the Word of God in very similar terms, as he wrote:

"For the word of God is living and powerful, and sharper than any two-edged sword, piercing even to the division of soul and spirit, and of joints and marrow, and is a discerner of the thoughts and intents of the heart."
- Hebrews 4:12 NKJV

Again, it's compared to a sword used in battle, but it's actions are here described in more detail. The Word of God is declared to be *"alive and powerful"* meaning that it is dynamic and empowered by the Spirit of God in our hearts. It has the ability of *"piercing the division of soul and spirit"* meaning that the Word can divide between what is spiritual and soulish in my life. It can clearly show us where sin lies and where our hearts need to grow more spiritually. The Word of God is also a *"discerner of the thoughts and intents of the heart"* in that the Spirit uses it to expose my true feelings and thoughts, bringing about conviction and growth in my life.

The Scriptures not only have tremendous transformative power for our own private hearts, but also for situations around us in life. When Jesus was tempted in the desert, after fasting for forty day and nights, He used the Sword of the Spirit to combat satan and defeat him in a time of temptation. We read this in Matthew's account of it:

"Then Jesus was led up by the Spirit into the wilderness to be tempted by the devil. And when He had fasted forty days and forty nights, afterward He was hungry. Now when the tempter came to Him, he said, "If You are the

***Son of God, command that these stones become
bread." But He answered and said, "It is written,
'Man shall not live by bread alone, but by every
word that proceeds from the mouth of God.' "
- Matthew 4:1-4 NKJV***

Though opposed by satan himself, and though He
is God in the flesh, Christ still chose to use the Word
of God as His weapon against the enemy! When satan
attempted to deceive Him with lies, Jesus countered
him 3 times with statements of eternal truth from
God's Word. Like thrusting back with a sword in
open combat, Jesus shot back portions of Scripture
He had memorized from Deuteronomy. So effective
was this, that at the end of this encounter, not only
did Jesus emerge victorious, but satan fled away in
defeat. Such is the power of the Word of God when
it is spoken in faith, believed in the mind, and sub-
mitted to in the heart–it can drive the enemy away
and bring us victory!

In the longest chapter of the Bible, the psalmist
describes this very same thing in order to bring
about triumph in the heart of a believer. He writes:

***"Your word I have hidden in my heart,
That I might not sin against You."
- Psalm 119:11 NKJV***

The psalmist reminds us, there is much power
to be gained from "hiding" God's Word in your heart
by memorizing it, and recalling it in the moment of
temptation. It can be the "sword" to drive away the

lies and deception of the enemy, and lead _you_ to triumph over sin and temptation!

Not only does it have a dynamic effect in your heart personally, but the Word of God will also transform others externally. This happens when it's released into a community by being faithfully proclaimed by Christians and diligently taught in their churches. Jesus referenced the dynamic power of God's Word to free people when He said:

> *"If you abide in My word, you are My*
> *disciples indeed.*
> *And you shall know the truth, and the*
> *truth shall make you free."*
> *- John 8:31-32 NKJV*

This is precisely why we _must_ diligently follow and spread the Word of God, as we expand Christ's Kingdom: it alone has the power to set people free from sin, liberate them from satan, and bring them to Christ! After sharing the Gospel, the teaching and preaching of the Word of God is what enables believers to grow and mature as Christians and know Jesus Christ on a deeper level than anything else. As we seek to use our Time, Talents, and Treasures to invest in the Kingdom of Heaven, we should do everything we can to get the Word of God out to more of our communities, our cities, and our world. _This_ is where we should spend our energy and resources!

When a person comes into contact with good solid bible teaching, they can be transformed, set free, and truly begin to grow into the man or woman they are called to be in Christ. The psalmist described the dynamic effect of the Word of God in a person's life, when he wrote:

> ***"Blessed is the man..his delight is in the***
> ***law of the Lord,***
> ***And in His law he meditates day***
> ***and night. He shall be like a tree***
> ***Planted by the rivers of water,***
> ***That brings forth its fruit in its season,***
> ***Whose leaf also shall not wither;***
> ***And whatever he does shall prosper."***
> ***- Psalm 1:1-3 NKJV***

As a person spends time in the Scriptures, whether it's in reading, meditation, or deeper study, it will always bring tremendous positive benefits into their spiritual life. The psalmist says they'll be blessed, have the abiding strength of a tree, be refreshed continually by streams of spiritual water, be bearing fruit in the Lord, and prospering in their life in Christ. A believer could hardly ask for more than this! Yet it's all found by simply being continually exposed to, and immersed in the Word of God. This is why the Scriptures are one of the greatest tools that we can use in seeking to expand the Kingdom and live for Heaven!

Knowing the power of it, God Himself magnifies His written Word supremely. The psalmist writes these amazing words:

*"You have magnified Your word above
all Your name."
- Psalm 138:2 NKJV*

Absolutely incredible! The Lord magnifies His Word even above His own Holy Name. If we realize that the Name of the LORD appears over 7,000 times in the Scriptures, is not even dared to be pronounced by the Jews today, and that it is the Name above all other names, we suddenly understand how exalted the Word of God is in the heart of the Lord! His Words are intimately connected to His nature and character, and so are supremely magnified in this world!

The question, of course, is how much do *you* exalt the Word of God in your own personal life? How important do *you* think it is to get good solid Bible teaching out to the world around you? If the Lord Himself honors and magnifies His Word this greatly, shouldn't *you* as well?

Use the tool of God's Word as much as you can for the Kingdom of Heaven. Any chance you have to help the Word of God "run swiftly" through the world, go for it. It's one of the greatest investments you can make towards eternity, and a powerful way to expand and grow the Kingdom of God!

#4–Use the Tool of YOUR TESTIMONY for Christ's Kingdom

Lastly, another dynamic tool that God has committed into your care is that of your own personal "salvation story", otherwise known as your testimony. You may not think it has much power, but in reality, for some people this may be the most powerful tool you can use to draw them to Christ. As a matter of fact, there are numerous places in the Scriptures where we see individuals using their personal testimonies, to expose others around them to the Lord.

One of the most surprising examples is the Babylonian king, Nebuchadnezzar. Unbeknownst to many, he not only came to faith in the Living God (Daniel 3), but even went on to share his testimony with the people of his entire kingdom! He wrote a personal letter, that was to be dispersed throughout all of his empire, which began like this:

"Nebuchadnezzar the king, To all peoples, nations, and languages that dwell in all the earth: Peace be multiplied to you. I thought it good to declare the signs and wonders that the Most High God has worked for me."
- Daniel 4:1-3 NKJV

If you read the entire letter, you'll probably agree with most Bible teachers, that Nebuchadnezzar came to a saving knowledge of the Lord through the witness of Daniel and his friends. I wonder how many people in the kingdom of Babylon were impacted by this letter from their king, and who may have been drawn to the Lord as a consequence. We'll only know in eternity, but we can be sure, that a person's salvation story is one of the best tools they have for telling those around them about the Lord, and His great love!

In the New Testament, we see another man who shared his testimony, not just once, but on numerous occasions. He too, was a murderous man that was radically changed, and came to a saving knowledge of the Lord. His name was Saul, but it was soon changed to Paul after meeting the risen Jesus. The book of Acts records one occasion where Paul tried to use his testimony to bring his fellow Jews to Christ:

"So when he had given him permission, Paul stood on the stairs and motioned with his hand to the people. And when there was a great silence, he spoke to them in the Hebrew language, saying,"Brethren and fathers, hear my defense before you now." And when they heard that he spoke to them in the Hebrew language, they kept all the more silent. Then he said: "I am indeed a Jew, born in Tarsus of Cilicia, but brought up in this city at the feet of Gamaliel, taught according to the strictness of our fathers' law, and was zealous toward God as you all are today. I persecuted this Way to the death.."
- Acts 23:40-22:4 NKJV

Paul went on to recount for them how he was personally encountered and blinded by the risen Christ (Acts 9), and that he now knew, that Jesus was the Lord and Messiah sent to save us. Millions of people have been impacted by the power of Paul's conversion and testimony down through the ages. And the Lord wants to use *your* testimony the same way – to impact people and bring them closer to the Savior that loves them!

Sharing your testimony and telling someone what the Lord has done for you is actually very easy. You simply share 3 things with them:

1. **Who you were *before* Jesus**
2. **How Jesus *saved* you.**
3. **How Jesus has *changed* you since then.**

This is exactly what a legal witness does in a court of law. They simply report on what they have personally seen and experienced. Isn't it interesting, that this is what Jesus has called us to be for Him, as we go throughout this dark world...*witnesses!!* He said this to the disciples just before He ascended into Heaven:

> *"..you shall receive power when the Holy Spirit has come upon you; and you shall be witnesses to Me .. to the end of the earth."*
> *- Acts 1:8 NKJV*

So go ahead and be exactly that, a witness for Jesus Christ! Share your testimony whenever you can with those around you. Let them know what you were like before Christ, how Jesus saved you, and how He has radically changed you!

On a practical note, I encourage you to have multiple versions of your testimony that you can use: a 30 second version; a five-minute version; and a longer version. This will help you, depending on what situation you find yourself in, at a given moment. If you're in and elevator, use the 30 second version. If you find yourself on a four-hour flight, then you can take your time, and work in the long version over the course of the entire trip!

Regardless of how you choose to do it, be sure to practice sharing your testimony regularly with those around you. Your "salvation story" is a powerful tool the Lord has given you, and you can never tell how Jesus will use it to draw people to Himself. Use this tool, and you'll be making great investments for the Kingdom of Heaven!

The Conclusion:

O ne day, an American tourist visited an old Rabbi. He was astonished to see this Rabbi's home was just one single room and all it had in it were books, a table, and a bench. And so the tourist asked him, "Rabbi, where is your furniture?" And the Rabbi answered, "Where is yours?" "Mine? I'm just a visitor here. I'm only passing through." And the Rabbi said, "So am I."

This should be the attitude of every follower of Jesus Christ as well! Now that our study is complete, I hope you can understand the Doctrine of Heaven in it's entirety: the ***Dimension*** of Heaven, the ***Kingdom*** of Heaven, and the ***Eternal*** Heavens. I hope that you now understand how to practically live for Heaven on a daily basis: by using your ***Time***, your ***Talents***, your ***Treasures***, and your ***Tools*** to invest in the Kingdom of God. Now that our study is drawing to a close, only one question remains:

*"Will **you** choose to seek Heaven*
diligently and zealously?

I invite and challenge you to follow the advice of Florence Chadwick, the world record swimmer. Keep the "shoreline of Heaven" in clear view in your life. No matter what comes your way, no matter what you go through, no matter what transpires...*don't quit and don't give up!*

Keep *walking* with Jesus, keep *loving* Jesus, keep *worshipping* Jesus, and keep *serving* Jesus diligently and faithfully, knowing that you will soon stand before Him to be rewarded for a life lived in honor of Him and His Kingdom!

Like Paul the Apostle, seek to *run* a good race, *fight* a good fight, and *finish* your course until the very end. May the hope and reality of Heaven give you motivation, inspiration, and stir your imagination until the day that you come face to face with your King and Savior, Jesus Christ...*in His glorious Heaven!*

"Only One Life" by C.T. Studd
"Two little lines I heard one day,
Traveling along life's busy way;
Bringing conviction to my heart,
And from my mind would not depart;
Only one life, 'twill soon be past,
Only what's done for Christ will last!

Only one life, yes only one,
Soon will its fleeting hours be done;
Then, in 'that day' my Lord to meet,
And stand before His Judgement seat;
Only one life,'twill soon be past,
Only what's done for Christ will last!

Oh let my love with fervor burn,
And from the world now let me turn;
Living for Thee, and Thee alone,
Bringing Thee pleasure on Thy throne;
Only one life, "twill soon be past,
Only what's done for Christ will last!

CPSIA information can be obtained
at www.ICGtesting.com
Printed in the USA
FSOW04n0050311016
26790FS

9 781498 481816